First Certificate:Fi

Examination Practice 2

Listening and Speaking

by Steven Bower and
Chris Wilson

Express Publishing

First Certificate:First!

Examination Practice 2: Listening and Speaking

Steven Bower - Chris Wilson

Published by Express Publishing 2001

Liberty House, New Greenham Park, Newbury, Berkshire RG19 6HW
Tel: (0044) 1635 817 363 - Fax: (0044) 1635 817 463
e-mail: inquiries@expresspublishing.co.uk
http://www.expresspublishing.co.uk

Components

Student's Book   ISBN   1-84325-002-0
Teacher's Book   ISBN   1-84325-003-9

Contents

To the Teacher

First Certificate:First! Examination Practice 2 uses the same novel approach as Examination Practice 1 to prepare candidates for the First Certificate in English examination.

Two Volumes, consisting of five complete practice tests for all Papers in the new revised FCE test format:

Volume 1: Reading, Writing, Use of English
Volume 2: Listening and Speaking

Tests include:
Detailed Task Analysis and Description: instructions to the student as to what each Part of each Paper is about and how to complete it.

Step-by-Step Guidance: checklists with specific steps for each Part of the Paper.

Time Management Tips: total time for each Paper as well as suggested time for each Part.

Guidance Questions: questions designed to help the students reach the correct answers.

Difficulty Monitor: a monitor which the students can use to indicate the level of difficulty for each Part of the test and get help in the required areas.

Two Teacher's books, one for each Volume, contain the answers to the tests as well as the answers to the Guidance Questions.

Available with Volume 2 is a set of audio cassettes/Cds for the Listening Paper, based on the actual Cambridge FCE format.

We know that First Certificate:First! will make learning easier and rewarding for both students and teachers.

To the Student

As the time approaches for you to take the Cambridge FCE examination, you must be feeling some anxiety.

First Certificate:First! has been specially designed to help you understand and feel comfortable with the Revised FCE format.

There are two books with five separate tests for each Paper. The first one deals with Reading, Writing and the Use of English Papers. The second with Listening and Speaking. In each Part you will find contemporary topics and helpful hints to keep you interested and guide you to the right answers.

For each Part of each test there is a Detailed Task Analysis and Description which will instruct you in what you are to do and how to complete the task.

Time Management Tips will help you time yourself to make sure you complete the individual task and each Paper on time.

Checklists will remind you of the various steps you can take in each task.

Guidance Questions in each Part of the test will help you reach the right conclusion.

A Difficulty Monitor will help to remind you which exercises you felt were easy or difficult, so you can get additional assistance if you need it, and monitor your performance.

First Certificate:First! will be a new experience in learning. An interesting, fun and easy way to achieve your goal.

Good Luck!

TOTAL TIME
40 min.

Part 1 Suggested time: about 10 min.

What do you have to do in Part 1 of Paper 4?

Question 1

A. How will Mary be treated differently?
given more flexibility with assignment deadlines
B. Is this mentioned?
No

C. What will people start to do?
hand in work late

Question 2

A. Do you hear words relevant to a cooker?
yes-temperature

B. Do you hear words relevant to a washing machine?
yes-drum, temperature, buttons, automatic, powder
C. Do you hear words relevant to a toaster?
no

Question 3

A. How does the shop assistant respond to the request?
with questions

B. Is the customer serious?
yes

C. Does the assistant do anything to help the customer?
yes- he shows him an omelette pan

Question 4

A. How do we get a meal in a restaurant?
a waiter takes the orders
B. When do we decide what to eat on a picnic?
in advance
C. Is he going to cook?
no

You will hear people talking in eight different situations. For questions **1 - 8** choose the best answer **A**, **B** or **C**.

---

1 Listen to a woman talking to a colleague.
Why doesn't she want people to find out about Mary?

A People will want the same treatment as Mary.

B People will start to feel sorry for Mary.

C People will start to treat Mary differently.

A	1

2 You hear a man talking to his daughter.
What is the problem?

A He can't work the cooker.

B He can't work the washing machine.

C He can't work the toaster.

B	2

3 Listen to a dialogue in a shop.
What is the situation?

A The assistant doesn't understand what the customer wants.

B The assistant doesn't think the customer is being serious.

C The assistant doesn't seem willing to help the customer.

A	3

4 Listen to someone organising a meal.
Where is he?

A in a restaurant

B on a picnic

C at home

C	4

TOTAL TIME
40 min.

5 Listen to a man describing some physical symptoms.
What worries him most?

A He's not sure how serious his problem is.

B He's not sure which doctor to go to.

C He's not sure why the pain goes away.

A	5

6 Listen to a student phoning a friend about an assignment.
What can't she organise?

A her thoughts

B her time

C her notes

B	6

7 You hear a woman answer the doorbell.
What does the man want?

A to save a cat

B to get his cat

C to visit a friend

B	7

8 Listen to the same woman the following day.
How does she feel about her behaviour?

A She behaved foolishly.

B She behaved rudely.

C She behaved wisely.

C	8

Question 5

A. Does he express any thoughts about this?

He doesn't know 'what on earth's wrong'.

B. Does he mention different types of doctors?

no

C. Does the pain go away?

It goes away when he moves around.

Question 6

A. Does she know what she has to write?

yes- an assignment

B. Does she need to organise her time?

yes

C. Does she mention her notes?

no

Question 7

A. Is the cat in danger?

no

B. Where is the cat?

in the entrance hall

C. Does his friend live there?

no

Question 8

A. Does she say this?

no

B. Is she sorry she behaved the way she did?

no

C. Does she sound glad she behaved the way she did?

yes-she says 'you can't be too careful'

TEST 1

How difficult was this part?

EASY				DIFFICULT
1	2	3	4	5

Paper 4: Listening

Part 2 Suggested time:about 7 MIN.

What do you have to do in Part 2 of Paper 4?

9. What sort of word/ phrase would you expect here?

adjective

10. What information do you expect after 'cooked for'?

length of time

11. How is Chinese food cooked?

over a high heat

12. What should cooked vegetables be like?

crisp and colourful

13. What image did Chinese restaurants use to have?

a cheap place to eat

14-15. Listen for words describing how people are today.

adventurous, demanding

16. Is The Dynasty popular?

yes

17-18. What 'old' favourites are mentioned?

sweet and sour pork and Peking duck

You will hear a radio interview with the manager of a Chinese restaurant. She is talking about Chinese food in Britain now and in the past. For questions **9 - 18** complete the interviewer's notes. Write a word or short phrase in each box.

Chinese food became popular because British food used to

be | bland/boring | **9** .

Real Chinese food is cooked for | a very short time | **10** over a

very | high heat | **11** .

In Chinese cooking vegetables mustn't be | soft and mushy | **12** .

People in Britain used to consider Chinese restaurants as

| cheap | **13** places to eat.

Now, people are more | adventurous | **14** and

| (more) demanding | **15** .

The Dynasty is an expensive and a | very successful | **16**

restaurant.

In addition to the old favourites The Dynasty serves

| seafood | **17** and | vegetarian | **18**

dishes.

8

Suggested time: about 6 MIN. **Part 3**

TOTAL TIME
40 MIN.

You will hear five different people talking about their first experience away from home. For questions **19 - 23**, choose from the list **A - F** what the speaker felt. Use the letters only once. There is one extra letter which you don't need to use.

A I felt like I hadn't left.

B I don't feel it was good for me.

C I left home because I had to.

D I had a wonderful experience.

E I knew very little about life.

F I wasn't away for very long.

Speaker 1	E	19
Speaker 2	B	20
Speaker 3	F	21
Speaker 4	C	22
Speaker 5	A	23

What do you have to do in Part 3 of Paper 4?

A. What changes when you live alone? responsibility, independence, etc.

B. Who thought it was more negative than positive? speaker 2

C. Who was happy at home? speaker 4

D. Who uses extremely positive language? no-one

E. Who didn't expect problems? speaker 1

F. Who sounds disappointed? speaker 3

Paper 4: Listening

Part 4 *Suggested time:about* 10 MIN.

What do you have to do in Part 4 of Paper 4?

You will hear a conversation in a bookshop. For questions **24 - 30**, decide whether the following statements are True(**T**) or False (**F**).

24. How does he respond when the customer tells him the title?
He doesn't seem to recognize it.

25. Has the customer visited other bookshops?
Yes-he's been to 'every bookshop in town'.

26. How else can we express 'variety' (or its opposite)?
a collection of different things; similarity, uniformity

27. In what other ways can we express 'popular' (or its opposite)?
in demand, well liked; unusual, uncommon, unliked

28. Does the shop assistant recommend a book?
no

29. What is a 'discount'?
a reduction in the normal price

30. In what ways can a book be damaged?
torn, marked, etc.

24 The shop assistant doesn't know the book.

T	24

25 This is the first bookshop the customer has visited.

F	25

26 The bookshop has a variety of books for learning languages.

T	26

27 The book is very popular.

F	27

28 The shop assistant recommended the book.

F	28

29 The shop assistant will reduce the price.

T	29

30 The book is damaged.

T	30

EASY   DIFFICULT
1 2 3 4 5 | *How difficult was this part?*

My Progress
Listening Test One

Areas I had difficulty with:

In Part 1:_____
In Part 2:_____
In Part 3:_____
In Part 4:_____

Areas I found easy:

In Part 1:_____
In Part 2:_____
In Part 3:_____
In Part 4:_____

Things to remember:

In Part 1:_____
In Part 2:_____
In Part 3:_____
In Part 4:_____

Things to listen for:

In Part 1:_____
In Part 2:_____
In Part 3:_____
In Part 4:_____

TOTAL TIME
40 MIN.

Part 1 *Suggested time: about 10 MIN.*

What do you have to do in Part 1 of Paper 4?

You will hear people talking in eight different situations. For questions **1 - 8** choose the best answer **A**, **B** or **C**.

Question 1

A. What is needed for quality work?
time
B. Does the man want to make changes?
no
C. Why is 'money' mentioned?
they want to make money

1 You hear a man talking about an exhibition.
What does he want the listener to do?

A improve the quality of work

B stop asking for changes

C lend him some money

B	1

Question 2

A. Do you hear the number 1,000? What does it refer to?
yes- it refers to points
B. What is 'cappuccino'?
a type of coffee
C. What do you need to win a car?
1,000 or more points

2 You hear a quiz show presenter give a contestant his prize.
What is the prize?

A £ 1,000 in cash

B a coffee machine

C a luxury car

B	2

Question 3

A. Do you think the incident is possible?
no
B. Are the events logical?
no
C. Are dreams always logical?
no

3 Listen to a woman describing an incident.
What is she describing?

A a true memory

B a live news report

C a strange dream

C	3

Question 4

A. What other expressions can we use for 'too small'?
'not enough room'

B. In what context is Sweden mentioned?
a phone call from Sweden

C. What does the speaker say about moving?
'if I've moved'

4 You hear a woman talking to a friend.
What is the problem?

A Her flat is too small.

B She will be in Sweden.

C She will be moving.

A	4

5 You hear a teacher talking about a student.
What is the problem?

A He is foolish.

B He is arrogant.

| B | 5 |

C He is violent.

6 Listen to part of a telephone conversation.
What does the caller want most?

A fruit

B flowers

| C | 6 |

C toiletries

7 Listen to a conversation between a man and a woman.
What does the man want?

A to thank her for helping

B to borrow her car

| A | 7 |

C to sell her his furniture

8 Listen to a telephone conversation.
What does the caller want?

A to speak to the operator

B to order a taxi

| B | 8 |

C to order a pizza

Question 5

A. How do foolish people behave?
unwisely

B. How do arrogant people behave?
They think they are always right.

C. How would this affect the other students.
They would be afraid.

Question 6

A. Is fruit mentioned?
yes

B. Does the caller need flowers?
no

C. What are toiletries?
soap, toothpaste,etc...

Question 7

A. How can we thank someone?
with words or with actions

B. Is the car mentioned?
yes

C. Is the man selling his furniture?
no

Question 8

A. Is the operator mentioned?
yes

B. How do you order a taxi?
you phone the taxi company

C. Is pizza mentioned?
no

TEST 2

Part 2 *Suggested time:about 7 MIN.*

You will hear an editor presenting a new dictionary. For questions **9 - 18** complete the Press Release. Write a word or short phrase in each box.

What do you have to do in Part 2 of Paper 4?

9. **What kind of word do you expect here?**

a verb

10. **What is another word for idea?**

concept

11. **What is 'jargon'?**

expressions used by a particular profession or group

12. **What kinds of words do you expect here?**

adjectives

13. **What is needed to ensure accuracy of entries?**

research

14. **What aspects of language are mentioned?**

words and meaning

15. **Which two subjects are mentioned as a pair?**

Science and Technology

16. **What sort of changes are most relevant?**

recent changes

17. **What language skills are mentioned?**

speaking, reading and writing

18. **Which two qualities are mentioned?**

confidence and authority

Heritage Press

PRESS RELEASE

Heritage Press has published a dictionary entitled the 'New English Dictionary'. The publishers | predict/believe **9** | that it will make its mark in the highly competitive field of language reference publications now and in the future.

Firstly, the | concept **10** | is new. Jargon-free English avoids confusion, and ensures exceptional | clarity **11** | . The novel page design offers | quick and easy **12** | access.

Secondly, extensive language | research **13** | guarantees that the entries reflect thousands of new words and their | meanings **14** | , for example in the world of Science and | Technology **15** | . Information on | recent **16** | changes in usage and a guide to pronunciation are also included to enable the user to | speak, read and write **17** | with confidence and | authority **18** | .

You will hear five different people who all saw the same play. For questions **19 - 23**, choose from the list **A - F** what each one says about the experience. Use the letters only once. There is one extra letter which you do not need to use.

What do you have to do in Part 3 of Paper 4?

A liked the performance and the costumes

B didn't like the performance, but found the music interesting

C didn't like anything about the performance

D didn't like the performance, but thought the costumes were acceptable

E is confused because it was nothing like what he had expected

F is tired of watching this play, but didn't mind the costumes

Speaker 1	C	19
Speaker 2	E	20
Speaker 3	A	21
Speaker 4	D	22
Speaker 5	F	23

A. **Who sounds very positive?**
speaker 3

B. **Who is negative, but says a few positive things about the music?**
no one

C. **Who sounds completely negative?**
speaker 1

D. **Who is negative, but says a few positive things about the costumes?**
speaker 4

E. **Who expresses confusion?**
speaker 2

F. **Who speaks about the play in general, rather than the performance?**
speaker 5

TEST 2

Part 4 *Suggested time:about 10 min.*

You will hear a conversation between a husband and wife. For questions **24 - 30**, decide whether the following statements are True (**T**) or False (**F**).

What do you have to do in Part 4 of Paper 4?

24. **Why does the man mention mineral water?**
His company lost the contract.

25. **How does the woman sound?**
bored

26. **How else can we express this?**
get the sack, dismissed, fired

27. **Is a villa mentioned? What does the woman say about it?**
yes – sell it.

28. **What expression is used for 'a lot of money'?**
'loads of money'

29. **Has anyone won it? Who?**
Yes – the woman

30. **What does she say about a new car?**
She will probably buy a new car.

24 The man works for a mineral water company. | F | 24 |

25 The woman is not interested in what the man is saying. | T | 25 |

26 The man has just lost his job. | T | 26 |

27 The man wants to buy a villa. | F | 27 |

28 The man has a lot of money. | T | 28 |

29 They have won the lottery. | F | 29 |

30 The woman has bought a new car. | F | 30 |

EASY   DIFFICULT
1 2 3 4 5 | *How difficult was this part?*

TOTAL TIME
40 MIN.

My Progress
Listening Test Two

Areas I had difficulty with:

In Part 1:_____
In Part 2:_____
In Part 3:_____
In Part 4:_____

Areas I found easy:

In Part 1:_____
In Part 2:_____
In Part 3:_____
In Part 4:_____

Things to remember:

In Part 1:_____
In Part 2:_____
In Part 3:_____
In Part 4:_____

Things to listen for:

In Part 1:_____
In Part 2:_____
In Part 3:_____
In Part 4:_____

Paper 4: Listening

TOTAL TIME
40 min.

Part 1 *Suggested time: about 10 min.*

What do you have to do in Part 1 of Paper 4?

You will hear people talking in eight different situations. For questions **1 - 8** choose the best answer **A**, **B** or **C**.

Question 1

What was wrong with the exhibition?
it was crowded with flowers and plants/it was humid

1 Listen to a man complaining about an exhibition.
What was exhibited?

  A hi-fi equipment

  B flowers & plants | A | 1 |

  C cars & boats

Question 2

What does the woman want to buy?
coconut milk and lemon grass

2 You hear a woman asking for information.
What shop has she called?

  A a delicatessen

  B a supermarket | A | 2 |

  C a restaurant

Question 3

What do the key words relate to?
acting-act three, scene

3 Listen to a woman talking about Sally & George.
Who are they?

  A colleagues at work

  B friends of hers | C | 3 |

  C characters in a play

Question 4

What do you buy/do in each of them?
A-deposit or withdraw money
B-buy stamps, post mail
C-buy groceries

4 You will hear a conversation in a queue.
Where are the people?

  A bank

  B post office | B | 4 |

  C supermarket

5 You will hear a conversation in a supermarket.
What is wrong?

A The customer wasn't at the right till.

B The customer didn't have enough money.

| A | 5 |

C The customer hadn't bought enough things.

Question 5
Which two answers are incorrect?
B–had a chequebook
C–had too many things

6 You will hear two people talking.
How are they going to travel?

A by coach

B by train

| B | 6 |

C by plane

Question 6
What key words indicate how they will travel?
'rocking and rhythmic sound, buffet car, platform'

7. Listen to a woman talking.
What is she talking about?

A her pet dog

B her grandson

| A | 7 |

C her neighbour

Question 7
What key words do you hear?
'soft barks, wagging his tail, thoroughbred, master'

8. You hear two girls talking about a test.
What sort of test is it?

A mathematics

B sociology

C personality

| C | 8 |

Question 8
Where would you take a mathematics test?
in school; under exam conditions

TEST 3

How difficult was this part? | EASY DIFFICULT 1 2 3 4 5 |

Part 2 Suggested time:about 7 min.

What do you have to do in Part 2 of Paper 4?

9. What is the main problem?
panic

10. What happens as a result of this problem?
You don't understand everything.

11. What should we learn to listen for?
the overall meaning

12. What else should we learn how to listen for?
particular details

13. What can affect your listening?
(background) noise

14. How should you prepare for listening?
by reading the questions first

15-16. What could be included in the 'overall meaning'?
emotions, main topic, etc.

17. What is another word for exact?
specific

18. What should you do after reading the questions?
guess what you will be listening for

Listen to a student teacher, Chris, talking to an older teacher, Margaret, about the difficulties students face with listening tasks. For questions **9 - 18**, complete the notes. Write a word or a short phrase in each box.

Don't | panic | **9** | !

Don't | expect to understand | **10** | every word.

Do listen for the | overall meaning | **11** | or for

| particular | **12** | details.

Don't pay attention to | background noise | **13** | on the cassette.

Do | look at/read the questions | **14** | before you listen.

Do listen for overall meaning such as how | the speakers are feeling | **15**

or the | topic of conversation | **16** | .

Do listen for | specific information | **17** | such as dates, times,

names and places.

Do try to | guess | **18** | the kind of information you will be

listening for.

EASY   DIFFICULT
1 2 3 4 5 | *How difficult was this part?*

You will hear five different people talking about occasions when a disaster was avoided. For questions **19 - 23**, choose from the list **A - F** which speaker matches each description. There is one extra letter that you do not need to use.

What do you have to do in Part 3 of Paper 4?

A over-estimated the danger

B prevented a fire

C under-estimated the danger

D was rescued from a fire

E had a small amount of damage

F was shocked

Speaker 1	B	19
Speaker 2	E	20
Speaker 3	A	21
Speaker 4	F	22
Speaker 5	C	23

A. Who imagined the worst?
speaker **3**

B. What is a common cause of house fires?
cooking

C. Who was not directly involved?
speaker **5**

D. Were any of the speakers in a fire?
no

E. Who spotted the damage in time?
speaker **2**

F. Who was still upset after the incident?
speaker **4**

TEST 3

Paper 4: Listening

Part 4 Suggested time: about 10 min.

What do you have to do in Part 4 of Paper 4?

You will hear a person being interviewed for a job. For questions **24 - 30**, put a **(Y)** for **Yes** or **(N)** for **No** next to each statement.

24. What is the appli-
    cant's full name?
    Peter Mortimer Jones

24 His first name is Mortimer. | N | 24 |

25. What does Jones
    say?
    '30 actually'

25 He is thirty one years old. | N | 25 |

26. What degrees are
    mentioned?
    BA and Masters

26 He has a degree in Economics. | Y | 26 |

27. What does 'import-
    export' refer to in the
    interview?
    a department at the bank

27 He has worked for an import - export company. | N | 27 |

28. What cities has Jones
    worked in?
    Manchester and London

28 He has worked in Germany. | N | 28 |

29. What is another word
    for plenty in this
    case?
    'substantial'

29 He has plenty of experience. | Y | 29 |

30. How do we know
    this?
    thesis on high-risk loans,
    working experience

30 He has specialised in loans. | Y | 30 |

EASY   DIFFICULT
1 2 3 4 5 | *How difficult was this part?*

TOTAL TIME
40 min.

My Progress
Listening Test Three

Areas I had difficulty with:

In Part 1:_____
In Part 2:_____
In Part 3:_____
In Part 4:_____

Areas I found easy:

In Part 1:_____
In Part 2:_____
In Part 3:_____
In Part 4:_____

Things to remember:

In Part 1:_____
In Part 2:_____
In Part 3:_____
In Part 4:_____

Things to listen for:

In Part 1:_____
In Part 2:_____
In Part 3:_____
In Part 4:_____

TEST 3

TOTAL TIME
40 min.

Part 1 *Suggested time: about 10 min.*

What do you have to do in Part 1 of Paper 4?

You will hear people talking in eight different situations. For questions **1 - 8** choose the best answer **A**, **B** or **C**.

Question 1

What is the typical response to each of these films?
A – curiosity
B – terror
C – laughter

1 Listen to a woman talking about a film.
   What sort of film was it?

   A science-fiction

   B horror

   C comedy

   | B | 1 |

Question 2

How does the woman's boss speak to her?
like a naughty child

2 Listen to a woman talking to a colleague.
   What is she complaining about?

   A the boss's computer

   B the boss's manner

   C the boss's child

   | B | 2 |

Question 3

What expression is used to talk about how the pub changed?
'gone downhill'

3 Listen to a man talking about a pub.
   What is his opinion?

   A It used to be better.

   B It used to be cheaper.

   C It used to be worse.

   | A | 3 |

Question 4

What is another word for 'pills'?
tablets

4 Listen to a doctor giving advice to a patient.
   What doesn't he recommend?

   A holiday

   B rest

   C pills

   | C | 4 |

5 Listen to two colleagues.
Who owes the other money?

A the woman

B the man

C	5

C neither

Question 5

Is the woman serious or joking?
joking

6 Listen to a woman talking to a friend on the phone.
What is her problem?

A She doesn't know what to cook.

B She doesn't like vegetarian food.

A	6

C She doesn't know how to cook.

Question 6

Does she ask for general cooking advice?
no

Question 7

Listen to her voice – what does she seem to need?
to be left alone

7 Listen to a woman talking.
What does she want?

A to listen to music

B to be left alone

B	7

C to have a bath

Question 8

What are the 'two points'? Who are they relevant to?
using the photocopier, being absent
new students

8 Listen to a man talking to a group of people.
Who are they?

A new office staff

B new teachers

C	8

C new students

TEST 4

How difficult was this part? EASY DIFFICULT 1 2 3 4 5

25

Part 2 *Suggested time: about 7 MIN.*

What do you have to do in Part 2 of Paper 4?

You will hear a radio programme on vitamins. For questions **9 - 18**, complete the leaflet. Write a word or short phrase in each box.

9. Are vitamins and minerals the same?

no

10-11. Which vitamins are associated with fat and which with water?

fat: A,D,E,K water: B,C

12. What is the main characteristic of each group?

fat soluble: the body can store them

water soluble: the body can't store them

13. What is one of the main functions of vitamins?

to help metabolise proteins, carbohydrates and fats

14. Does the speaker give details about how vitamins work?

no

15-16. What sources of food can you think of?

plants and animals

17. Where is vitamin B-12 found?

in animal products

18. What does the speaker warn us about?

not to take more vitamins than we need

VITAMINS

Vitamins are important for a healthy body. Vitamins are [different from **9**] minerals.

There are two groups of vitamins:
· vitamins A, D, E & K, which are [fat soluble **10**].
· vitamins B and C, which are [water soluble **11**].

The human body cannot store vitamins B and C, so they must be included in our [daily diet **12**].

Without vitamins our body cannot process carbohydrates, [proteins and fats **13**], which are essential for life.

We don't know much about how vitamins [operate in the body **14**].

To get the vitamins we need, we should go for a balanced diet of [plant products **15**] such as fresh fruit and vegetables; vegetable oil and margarine; bread, cereals & pasta; as well as [animal products **16**] like dairy products - milk, butter and cheese; meat, poultry & fish.

[Vegetarians **17**] need to take B12 supplements.

Be careful when taking vitamin supplements! Unnecessary amounts can cause [health problems **18**].

EASY   DIFFICULT
1 2 3 4 5 | How difficult was this part?

Suggested time: about 6 *min.* **Part 3**

You will hear five different answerphone messages. For questions **19 - 23**, choose from the list **A - F** the reason each person missed an appointment. Use the letters only once. There is one extra letter which you do not need to use.

What do you have to do in Part 3 of Paper 4?

A. Who mentions damage to the car?
speaker 3

A had a car accident

B. What does 'get stuck' mean?
be unable to move

B got stuck in traffic

Speaker 1	F	19
Speaker 2	B	20
Speaker 3	A	21
Speaker 4	E	22
Speaker 5	C	23

C. What are the likely results?
being late

C didn't hear the alarm clock

D. What would you do if you missed the bus?
find a different means of transport

D missed the bus

E. Which speaker arrived too early?
speaker 4

E went there too early

F. How can this happen?
misunderstanding, forget the name of the place

F went to the wrong place

Part 4 *Suggested time: about 10 MIN.*

What do you have to do in Part 4 of Paper 4?

You will hear a radio interview with the owner of a new video-store chain. For questions **24 - 30** choose the best answer **A**, **B**, or **C**.

24. **What services do conventional video stores offer?**
videos for rent/sale

24 Computer Video Rental stores offer
  A the same services as conventional video stores.
  B different services from conventional video stores.
  C fewer services than conventional video stores.

| B | 24 |

25. **What do customers do when they don't know how to use the computers?**
ask the staff for help

25 The computers in the store can be used by
  A trained staff only.
  B customers only.
  C staff or customers.

| C | 25 |

26. **What is not mentioned?**
the soundtrack

26 The computer has not got information about
  A the protagonists.
  B the soundtrack.
  C the year of release.

| B | 26 |

27. **What example does Mulligan give?**
'type thriller and some key words'

27 To find a film you have to know
  A the type of film and words related to the story.
  B the names of some actors and the director.
  C some of the information stored in the computer.

| A | 27 |

28. **How long does home delivery take?**
around 30 minutes

28 When members ask for home delivery, they
  A have to pay extra.
  B get a free pizza.
  C wait for an hour.

| A | 28 |

29. **How many days do the stores close for?**
One and a half

29 Computer Video Rental stores close for
  A twenty-four hours.
  B twenty-four days.
  C thirty-six hours.

| C | 29 |

30. **Which of them are mentioned throughout the interview?**
video tapes and laser discs

30 In Computer Video Rental stores, customers can find
  A video tapes & laser disks.
  B video tapes & CDs.
  C video tapes, laser disks & CDs.

| A | 30 |

TOTAL TIME
40 min.

My Progress
Listening Test Four

Areas I had difficulty with:

In Part 1:_____
In Part 2:_____
In Part 3:_____
In Part 4:_____

Areas I found easy:

In Part 1:_____
In Part 2:_____
In Part 3:_____
In Part 4:_____

Things to remember:

In Part 1:_____
In Part 2:_____
In Part 3:_____
In Part 4:_____

Things to listen for:

In Part 1:_____
In Part 2:_____
In Part 3:_____
In Part 4:_____

Paper 4: Listening

Part 1 *Suggested time:about* 10 min.

What do you have to do in Part 1 of Paper 4?

You will hear people talking in eight different situations. For questions **1 - 8** choose the best answer **A**, **B** or **C**.

Question 1
How do cats ruin furniture?
They scratch it with their claws.

1 Listen to someone talking about her cat.
What is the problem?

   A The cat is often ill.

   B The cat is a responsibility. | B | 1 |

   C The cat ruins the furniture.

Question 2
What electronic equipment is mentioned?
the cable phone, the radio

2 Listen to a radio programme about an invention.
What invention is it?

   A mobile phone

   B cable television | A | 2 |

   C portable radio

Question 3
What key phrase points you to who is speaking?
'Can we come to some arrangement?'

3 Listen to a woman describing a flat.
Who is she?

   A the cleaner

   B the tenant | C | 3 |

   C the landlady

Question 4
What could happen when a printer breaks?
It won't print; it prints too dark or too light

4 Listen to two people talking in an office.
What are they talking about?

   A a computer

   B a photocopier | B | 4 |

   C a printer

5 Listen to a woman talking about a course she is taking.
What is her opinion?

A She thinks it is very boring.

B She is enjoying it very much.

C She doesn't like the teachers.

B	5

Question 5

How does the woman sound?
pleased (pleasantly surprised)

6 Listen to a secretary calling a customer.
What changes do they make?

A They changed the time.

B They changed the day.

C They changed the place.

A	6

Question 6

Does the customer live near the office?
no

Question 7

What key words do you hear?
spectators, referee, pool

7 Listen to a radio report.
What is it about?

A a live comedy show

B a ballet performance

C a water sports event

C	7

Question 8

In what circumstances can walking be quicker than driving?
when there is a lot of traffic

8 Listen to someone giving directions.
Which will be quicker?

A taxi

B bus

C foot

C	8

Part 2 *Suggested time:about* 7 MIN.

What do you have to do in Part 2 of Paper 4?

You will hear a lecture about dinosaurs. For questions **9 - 18** complete the notes which summarise the lecture. Write a word or short phrase in each box.

9. What are skeletons?
an arrangement of human or animal bones

10. What were dinosaurs?
reptiles

11. What other animal family is mentioned?
Mammal

12. What is a herbivore?
an animal that eats only plants

13. How do birds reproduce?
They lay eggs.

14. Did all dinosaurs have large brains?
no

15. What does extinct mean?
no longer exist

16. What theory is mentioned?
a meteor hitting the earth

17. What change occurred to the earth?
from a stable yearly climate to different seasons

18. What is meant by 'relatives' here?
directly descended from

Dinosaurs

Skeletons are also called | fossils | **9** |.

Dinosaurs were | reptiles | **10** | like snakes and lizards.

The Family of Dinosaurs is similar to the | Family of Mammals | **11** |.

Dinosaurs ate | meat or plants | **12** | and reproduced by

| laying eggs | **13** |.

Dinosaurs were as intelligent as the reptiles of today. Small, meat-eating dinosaurs

had the | largest brains | **14** |.

Dinosaurs disappeared | 65 million years ago | **15** |. There are two

possible reasons:

- the earth was | hit by a meteor | **16** |

- the earth's | climate changed | **17** |

The only living relatives of dinosaurs are | birds | **18** |.

EASY DIFFICULT
1 2 3 4 5 | *How difficult was this part?*

Suggested time:about 6 MIN. **Part 3**

You will hear five different people talking about a miracle. For questions **19 - 23**, choose from the list **A - F** how each of them feels. Use the letters only once. There is one extra letter which you do not need to use.

What do you have to do in Part 3 of Paper 4?

A The speaker thinks it is an optical illusion.

B The speaker doubts if miracles exist.

C The speaker disapproves of looking for miracles.

D The speaker thinks it is the result of suggestion.

E The speaker thinks it will help sick people.

F The speaker believes the miracle happened.

Speaker 1	F	19
Speaker 2	A	20
Speaker 3	D	21
Speaker 4	B	22
Speaker 5	C	23

A. **What is mentioned that can affect the eyes?**
heat and light from the candles

B. **Who is the most experienced in looking for miracles?**
speaker 4

C. **Who discusses wider issues?**
speaker 5

D. **Who talks about wanting something to happen?**
speaker 3

E. **Who talks about helping the sick?**
speaker 5

F. **Who doesn't try to explain?**
speaker 1

How difficult was this part? EASY DIFFICULT 1 2 3 4 5

TEST 5

TOTAL TIME
40 MIN.

Part 4 *Suggested time: about 10 MIN.*

What do you have to do in Part 4 of Paper 4?

24. What was different then?
it was mainly practical training

25. How do most people get paid?
pay cheque, cash

26. What has changed this?
going to college

27. Who was expecting something different?
Nick

28. What words are related to 'satisfaction'?
fulfilling

29. How do people show appreciation?
by saying thank you

30. Is an explanation given? What?
yes - 'traditionally nurses have been women'

You will listen to three people (Jane, Nick and Peggy) being interviewed about the nursing profession. For questions **24 - 30**, put a (**J**) for **Jane**, a (**P**) for **Peggy** or an (**N**) for **Nick** next to each question.

24 Who would like to have become a nurse 25 years ago?   P 24

25 Who is not satisfied with the money he/she earns?   J 25

26 Who says nurses are more respected now?   P 26

27 Who was disappointed when he/she started work?   N 27

28 Who says that he/she is satisfied with the job?   J 28

29 Who says a nurse's work is not always appreciated?   N 29

30 Who says it's normal for people to expect women nurses?   P 30

EASY   DIFFICULT
1 2 3 4 5 | *How difficult was this part?*

My Progress
Listening Test Five

Areas I had difficulty with:

In Part 1:_____
In Part 2:_____
In Part 3:_____
In Part 4:_____

Areas I found easy:

In Part 1:_____
In Part 2:_____
In Part 3:_____
In Part 4:_____

Things to remember:

In Part 1:_____
In Part 2:_____
In Part 3:_____
In Part 4:_____

Things to listen for:

In Part 1:_____
In Part 2:_____
In Part 3:_____
In Part 4:_____

FCE EXAMINATION PRACTICE

Listening

PART 1
TIME: Approx. 18 minutes. Questions and options are read aloud, which gives you about 20 seconds to think about the questions. You will hear each text twice, before you hear the next one.

TEXTS: 8 unrelated dramatic monologues or dialogues.

TASK: Multiple choice. For each question there are **3 options** to choose from. Only one answer is correct.

PART 2
TIME: Approx. 7 minutes. You have 45 seconds to look at the unfinished sentences. You will hear the text twice.

TEXT: One monologue or dialogue.

TASK: There are 10 questions. You are asked to complete sentences, fill in parts of a form, or answer questions. Write 1-4 words only!

PART 3
TIME: Approx. 6 minutes. You will hear the texts twice. You will hear all five texts together before they are repeated. You have 30 seconds to look at the statements before listening.

TEXT: 5 monologues by different people, related to the same topic.

TASK: Multiple matching. You are given 6 statements. You have to match each text or speaker to the statement that is true for the text/speaker. **One statement does not have a match.**

PART 4
TIME: Approx. 10 minutes. You will hear the text twice. You have 1 minute to look at the statements before listening.

TEXT: A conversation between 2 or more speakers.

TASK: 7 Questions; either **true/false** or **multiple choice**.

FCE EXAMINATION PRACTICE

Speaking

PART 1
TIME: approximately 3 minutes.

In Part 1 of Paper 5, the interlocutor will ask you some questions about your hobbies, family and friends in order to get to know you a little better and help to put you at ease.

PART 2
TIME: approximately 4 minutes.

In Part 2 of Paper 5, each candidate is asked to speak alone for about one minute. You will be given two pictures and asked to compare and contrast them.

PART 3
TIME: approximately 3 minutes.

In Part 3 of Paper 5, you will be speaking to your partner(s). The interlocutor will just listen. You will be asked to solve a problem. Each of you will be giving your opinions on the best solution to the problem. It is not necessary for you to agree.

PART 4
TIME: approximately 4 minutes.

In Part 4 of Paper 5, you, your partner(s) and the interlocutor will be talking together for about four minutes. You will be discussing themes similar to the ones you raised in part three.

TOTAL TIME

15 min.

Part 1 *Time for this part:* 3 min.

INTERVIEW

In Part 1 of Paper 5, the interlocutor will ask you some questions about what you like to do in your spare time.

 **Do**

... greet the interlocutor and assessor as you enter the room.

... think about your answers. What do you like to do? Why?

 **Don't**

... prepare a speech - this is a *conversation!*

HELP

What phrases and sounds do English speakers use to hesitate and give themselves time to think?

Group Work Activity

Work in groups of three.
One of you will be the *Interlocutor*, the person who talks to the candidates.
The other two will be the *Candidates*.

INTERLOCUTOR
Prepare some questions to ask your candidates about
- watching TV: favourite and least favourite types of programmes
- sports: favourite sports; what they like to play
- food: favourite and least favourite foods
- music: favourite and least favourite music

CANDIDATES
Look at the Do's and Don'ts on the left and think about your answers for Part One.

Carry out the interview.

What is your favourite television programme? Why?
What is your least favourite television programme? Why?

What is your favourite sport?
Do you prefer to watch or play?

What is your favourite food?
Can you cook?

What is your favourite music?
Who is your favourite singer?

EASY 1 2 3 4 5 DIFFICULT | *How difficult was this part?*

CANDIDATE A   Part 2 *Time for this part:* 4 min.

TOTAL TIME
15 min.

Pair Work Activity

ON YOUR OWN
Look at the two pictures.
How are they similar?
How are they different?
Who do you think took the photos?
Why do you think they were taken?
Would you like to be in either of the two places shown?

WITH A PARTNER
Candidate A:
Compare and contrast your pictures for your partner.
Candidate B:
Respond to your partner's ideas.

Where would you rather be?

INDIVIDUAL LONG TURN

In Part 2 of Paper 5, each candidate is asked to speak alone for about one minute. You will be given two pictures and asked to compare and contrast them.

✔ **Do**

... speak by yourself and not to the other candidate.

... listen to what your partner says: you will be asked to comment briefly at the end.

💣 **Don't**

... simply describe the pictures.

... panic if your mind goes blank.

Help

How many ways do you know of talking around a word you don't know or have forgotten?

EASY   DIFFICULT
How difficult was this part? | 1 2 3 4 5

TOTAL TIME
15 min.

Part 2 *Time for this part:* 4 min.

CANDIDATE B

INDIVIDUAL LONG TURN

In Part 2 of Paper 5, each candidate is asked to speak alone for about one minute. You will be given two pictures and asked to compare and contrast them.

Do

... speak by yourself and not to the other candidate.

... listen to what your partner says: you will be asked to comment briefly at the end.

Don't

... simply describe the pictures.

... panic if your mind goes blank.

Help

How many ways do you know of talking around a word you don't know or have forgotten?

Pair Work Activity

ON YOUR OWN
Look at the two pictures.
How are they similar?
How are they different?
Who do you think took the photos?
Why do you think they were taken?
Would you like to be in either of the two places shown?

WITH A PARTNER
Candidate A:
Compare and contrast your pictures for your partner.
Candidate B:
Respond to your partner's ideas.

Where would you rather be?

both are forms of recreation
both show people relaxing and enjoying themselves
one is a beach in summer, the other is a mountain in winter

EASY 1 2 3 4 5 DIFFICULT | *How difficult was this part?*

Part 3 *Time for this part:* 3 min.

Group Work Activity

CANDIDATES

You are planning to open a new fast food restaurant in the town you see in the picture. There are four places marked where you could open your restaurant.

Decide together which place you think would be the best, bearing in mind:

a) the age group you want to come to the restaurant

b) the times of day which will be the busiest

You don't have to agree. Discuss your plans for three minutes.

INTERLOCUTOR

Listen to the candidates and use the evaluation sheet to grade them. Tell the candidates how well they did and where they need improvement.

COLLABORATIVE TASK

In Part 3 of Paper 5, you will be speaking to your partner(s). The interlocutor will just listen. You will be asked to solve a problem. Each of you will be giving your opinions on the best solution to the problem. It is not necessary for you to agree.

Do

... remember that you must talk to the other candidate(s).

... ask for your partner's opinion.

Don't

... talk to the interlocutor during part three.

HELP

How many ways do you know of beginning a discussion?

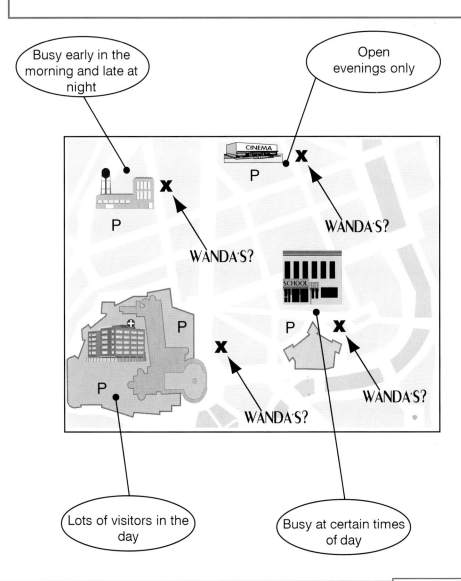

Busy early in the morning and late at night

Open evenings only

Lots of visitors in the day

Busy at certain times of day

CINEMA

WANDA'S?

WANDA'S?

SCHOOL

WANDA'S?

WANDA'S?

How difficult was this part? EASY 1 2 3 4 5 DIFFICULT

Paper 5: Speaking

Part 4 *Time for this part:* 4 MIN.

THREE-WAY DISCUSSION

In Part 4 of Paper 5, you, your partner(s) and the interlocutor will be talking together for about four minutes. You will be discussing themes similar to the ones you raised in part three.

Do

... give your own opinion.

... say 'goodbye' to the interlocutor and the assessor when you leave.

Don't

... dominate the conversation.

... interrupt or talk at the same time as the other candidate(s).

HELP

What ways do you know to disagree politely?

Group Work Activity

1) Work alone.
Answer the following questionnaire.

WANDA'S

Opening soon near you!
We want your opinions!

• How often do you go to fast food restaurants?

never	seldom	sometimes	regularly
☐	☐	☐	☐

• If you never go, tell us why.

....

• Do you think they are good value? Yes ☐ No ☐

• Which things are too expensive?

....

• Do you go for the food or the company?

....

• Do you think fast food is healthy? Yes ☐ No ☐

• What healthy foods do you like?

....

Thank you for completing this questionnaire!
WANDA'S
hopes to welcome you soon!

---

2) Work in groups of three.

INTERLOCUTOR
Ask questions and make comments that will keep the conversation flowing.

CANDIDATES
Give reasons for your opinions. How will the answers you have collected be useful to a fast food restaurant?

EASY ... DIFFICULT
1 2 3 4 5 | *How difficult was this part?*

TOTAL TIME
15 MIN.

Speaking - Test One
Personal Progress Record

I feel good about:

I need to practise:

USEFUL HINTS

☀ **Ways to give yourself time to think:**

speak slowly
use phrases like   'I think...'
                    'In reference to...'

☀ **Ways to 'talk around' words:**

describe the object/activity
give an example of the object/activity

PERSONAL PROGRESS RECORD

Use this record to keep notes on the following:

1. The aspects of the speaking test that you feel confident with.

2. The aspects of the speaking test that you feel you need to work on.

3. Useful language items that you can use to help yourself during the speaking test.

TOTAL TIME
15 min.

Part 1 *Time for this part: 3 min.*

In Part 1 of Paper 5, the interlocutor will ask you some questions about the subjects you study at school.

Do

... think about what the interlocutor might ask.

Don't

... worry if you don't understand everything the interlocutor says.

HELP

What ways do you know of asking someone to clarify something you didn't understand?

Group Work Activity

1) Work alone.
List below the school subjects you are very good at, the ones you are quite good at and the ones you find more difficult. Write possible reasons. Why are you better at some subjects than others?

I'm very good at	I'm good at
....	....
because	because
....	....
....	....

I find

....

more difficult because

....

....

2) Work in groups of three.
One of you will be the **Interlocutor** and the other two will be the **Candidates**.

INTERLOCUTOR
Ask the candidates about the subjects they find easiest and most difficult. Ask them what their reasons are.

CANDIDATES
Answer the Interlocutor's questions. Respond to what the other candidate has to say. Are there any similarities or differences in your results?

Carry out the interview.

I'm very good at English because I like learning new languages.

I'm good at history because I find it easy.

I find chemistry more difficult because I can't memorise the atomic table.

EASY DIFFICULT
1 2 3 4 5 | *How difficult was this part?*

CANDIDATE A **Part 2** Time for this part: 4 min.

Pair Work Activity

ON YOUR OWN
Look at the two pictures.
How are they similar?
How are they different?
Who do you think took the photos?
How do you think the children may be feeling?
Would you like to be in either of the two situations shown?

WITH A PARTNER
Candidate A:
Compare and contrast your pictures for your partner.
Candidate B:
Respond to your partner's ideas.

What memories of childhood do you have?

both show children looking happy and interested

in one the children are painting in the other the people are decorating a Christmas tree

one is of a family event; the other is possibly a school scene

In Part 2 of Paper 5, each candidate is asked to speak alone for about one minute. You will be given two pictures and asked to compare and contrast them.

 Do

... decide which picture you like best, and why.

 **Don't**

... panic if you realise you have made a mistake.

 **Help**

How can you correct yourself if you know you have made an error?

TEST 2

How difficult was this part? EASY DIFFICULT 1 2 3 4 5

Part 2 *Time for this part:* 4 min.

CANDIDATE B

INDIVIDUAL LONG TURN

In Part 2 of Paper 5, each candidate is asked to speak alone for about one minute. You will be given two pictures and asked to compare and contrast them.

 Do

... decide which picture you like best, and why.

 **Don't**

... panic if you realise you have made a mistake.

 **Help**

How can you correct yourself if you know you have made an error?

Pair Work Activity

ON YOUR OWN
Look at the two pictures.
How are they similar?
How are they different?
Who do you think took the photos?
What do you think the people are doing?
Would you like to be in either of the two situations shown?

WITH A PARTNER
Candidate A:
Compare and contrast your pictures for your partner.
Candidate B:
Respond to your partner's ideas.

What traditional dances do you know?

both show traditional costume
in one the participants are standing still, in the other they are moving
in one picture the participants seem relaxed, in the other they are concentrating and looking serious

EASY DIFFICULT
1 2 3 4 5 *How difficult was this part?*

Part 3 *Time for this part:* 3 *MIN.*

Group Work Activity

CANDIDATES
You have won a day trip to London. You will be arriving at nine in the morning, and you have to leave at midnight. Below are some of the places you could visit. Together, plan your day.

You don't have to agree. Discuss your plans for three minutes.

INTERLOCUTOR
Listen to the candidates and use the evaluation sheet to grade them. Tell the candidates how well they did and where they need improvement.

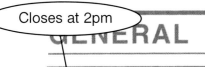
Closes at 2pm

GENERAL

Museums

THE TOWER OF LONDON
Built by William the Conqueror. It has been a castle, a prison, a museum. See the fabulous Crown Jewels!

The London Dungeon

London's Medieval Horror Museum and Torture Chamber.

Not for the faint-hearted!

Food

China Town
Hundreds of Superb Chinese Restaurants

Covent Garden
Dozens of fantastic Shops, Cafes and Restaurants!

Business Services

SECURITY, BODYGUARD, driver, translator (Arabic, French, English, Italian, & Polish). Tel: +49 (0) 171-84 65 115 or +49

Entertainment

THE WEST END

London's Theatre Land
Cats-Starlight Express
Les Miserables
Romeo and Juliet

and many more performances every evening.

Capital Available

UNLIMITED INT'L FUNDING
and Project Financ
Fax brief project s
364 or e-mail: successfu

Starts at 8pm, ends at 11:30pm

COLLABORATIVE TASK

In Part 3 of Paper 5, you will be speaking to your partner(s). The interlocutor will just listen. You will be asked to solve a problem. Each of you will be giving your opinions on the best solution to the problem. It is not necessary for you to agree.

✔ **Do**

... listen to your partner.

... encourage him/her to speak.

● **Don't**

... let your partner do all the talking.

HELP

What ways do you know to enter into a conversation politely?

How difficult was this part? | EASY DIFFICULT | 1 2 3 4 5

Paper 5: Speaking

Part 4 *Time for this part:* 4 MIN.

THREE - WAY DISCUSSION

In Part 4 of Paper 5, you, your partner(s) and the interlocutor will be talking together for about four minutes. You will be discussing themes similar to the ones you raised in part three.

Do

... say what you really feel.

... show interest in what others say.

Don't

... ignore the other candidate

... just respond to the interlocutor.

HELP

What ways do you know of showing interest in what someone is saying?

Group Work Activity

1) Work alone.
Think of the city you would most like to visit for one day, if you could. Below are some ideas to help you:

famous buildings to see

kinds of food to try

famous places to visit

national events to go to

London?...New York?... Paris?...
Tokyo?...Bombay?...Madrid?... Sydney?...Rome?...Athens?...
Los Angeles?... Bangkok?

2) Work in groups.
Tell each other about the city you have chosen. Can you convince anyone to come with you? Can anyone change your mind about your original choice?

EASY 1 2 3 4 5 DIFFICULT | *How difficult was this part?*

TOTAL TIME
15 min.

Speaking Test Two
Personal Progress Record

I feel good about:

I need to practise:

USEFUL HINTS

✳ Ways to correct yourself:

What I mean is...
I'm sorry, I was mistaken/wrong. Now...
I can see/realise that...

✳ Ways to enter a conversation politely:

Excuse me...
I believe/think that...
That's an interesting idea...

Use this record to keep notes on the following:

1. The aspects of the speaking test that you feel confident with.

2. The aspects of the speaking test that you feel you need to work on.

3. Useful language items that you can use to help yourself during the speaking test.

TEST 2

TOTAL TIME
15 MIN.

Part 1 *Time for this part:* 3 MIN.

INTERVIEW

What do you have to do in Part 1 of Paper 5?

Do

... think about what you would really like to do and why.

Don't

... worry if you have no specific plans yet: say so!

HELP

Think about the structures you can choose to talk about plans and wishes for the future.

Group Work Activity

1) Work alone.
Look at the suggestions in the box below. What would you like to do? What would you definitely not like to do? Write some questions to ask your classmates about their future plans.

2) Work in groups of three.
One of you will be the **Interlocutor** and the other two will be the **Candidates.**

INTERLOCUTOR
Interview the two candidates on what they would like to do.
Did you ask any questions apart from the ones you had prepared?

CANDIDATES
Answer the Interlocutor's questions. Include as many details as possible.
Did you have difficulty with specific words?
How did the conversation flow?

Carry out the interview.

Which would you like to be?
Which wouldn't you like to be?
Why?

Doctor

Lawyer

Journalist

Film star

Architect

Computer Programmer

Soldier

Other

✱ Family : Yes? No? Why?

✱ Money : Important? Why (not)?

✱ Satisfaction or wealth? Which is more important?

EASY DIFFICULT
1 2 3 4 5 *How difficult was this part?*

CANDIDATE A   Part 2 *Time for this part:* 4 MIN.

TOTAL TIME
15 MIN.

INDIVIDUAL LONG TURN

What do you have to do in Part 2 of Paper 5?

 Do

... imagine yourself in the photo -how would you feel?

 **Don't**

... panic if you don't immediately recognise what is happening in the photo - make some guesses.

**HELP**

How many ways do you know of expressing uncertainty in English?

TEST 3

Pair Work Activity

ON YOUR OWN
Look at the two pictures.
Write down as many words as you can that describe your feelings about the jobs and the possible feelings of the people in the photographs.

WITH A PARTNER
Candidate A:
Compare and contrast your photos for your partner. Include some or all of the words you wrote down.

Candidate B:
Respond to your partner's ideas.

Which job would you rather do?

Words
interested, obliged, involved, committed, concerned, dedicated, exciting, dangerous, etc.

How difficult was this part? EASY 1 2 3 4 5 DIFFICULT

TOTAL TIME
15 MIN.

Part 2 *Time for this part:* 4 MIN.

CANDIDATE B

INDIVIDUAL LONG TURN

What do you have to do in Part 2 of Paper 5?

Do

... imagine yourself in the photo - how would you feel?

Don't

... panic if you don't immediately recognise what is happening in the photo - make some guesses.

Help

How many ways do you know of expressing uncertainty in English?

Pair Work Activity

ON YOUR OWN
Look at the two pictures.
Write down as many words as you can that describe how you think the people in the photographs are feeling.

WITH A PARTNER
Candidate A
Compare and contrast your photos for your partner. Include some or all of the words you wrote down.

Candidate B
Respond to your partner's ideas.

Where would you rather be?

words:
relaxing, calm, balmy, serene, fun, hectic, noisy, thrilling, etc.

EASY 1 2   DIFFICULT 3 4 5 | *How difficult was this part?*

Part 3 *Time for this part:* 3 min.

Group Work Activity

CANDIDATES

These people have applied for the position of head of the school. Which of the three would you offer the post to and why?

You don't have to agree. Discuss your plans for three minutes.

INTERLOCUTOR

Listen to the candidates and use the evaluation sheet to grade them. Tell the candidates how well they did and where they need improvement.

COLLABORATIVE TASK

What do you have to do in Part 3 of Paper 5?

 Do

... make sure you are ready with reasons for your opinions.

 **Don't**

... say anything you cannot justify.

 *HELP*

What ways do you know of asking someone why they believe a certain thing?

TEST 3

HAMPSHIRE COUNTY SCHOOL

Patricia Lewis
Age 32
Chemistry teacher
Has written a school text book on chemistry
Believes in:
· discipline and respect
· weekly tests
· compulsory sports

James Fox
Age 56
Sports instructor
Coaches local football team
Believes in:
· need for pleasant school environment
· friendly relationships between students and staff
· importance of strong discipline.

Julia Nuttal
Age 35
Psychologist
Is writing a book about educational psychology
Believes in:
· freedom of self-expression
· respects differences of opinion
· encourages students to develop artistic talents

Part 4 *Time for this part:* 4 *min.*

**THREE - WAY
DISCUSSION**

**What do you have to do
in Part 4 of Paper 5?**

 Do

... give reasons for your
opinions.

 **Don't**

... sit in silence!

 *HELP*

Use all the ways you
have thought of so far
to keep a conversation
going.

Group Work Activity

1) Work alone.
Look at the statements below about good teachers. Write **A** for agree,
D for disagree or **?** for don't know, in the circle.

2) Work in groups of three.
Compare your answers. How many points do you agree/disagree on?
Give reasons for your opinions.

A GOOD TEACHER SHOULD:

○ be strict

○ give a lot of homework

○ never correct students

○ be a good friend to the students

○ be interested in the same things as the students

○ maintain high standards

○ keep a certain distance from the students

○ listen to the students' problems

○ know a lot about the subject

○ be up to date on teaching techniques

EASY		DIFFICULT			
1	**2**	**3**	**4**	**5**	*How difficult was this part?*

TOTAL TIME
15 min.

Speaking Test Three
Personal Progress Record

I feel good about:

I need to practice:

USEFUL HINTS

❋ Ways to express uncertainty:

I'm not sure, but...
It is possible that...
It is likely/unlikely...

❋ Ways to ask someone why they believe a certain thing:

That's interesting. What makes you think that?
Why do you say that?
Have you experienced...?

Use this record to keep notes on the following:

1. The aspects of the speaking test that you feel confident with.

2. The aspects of the speaking test that you feel you need to work on.

3. Useful language items that you can use to help yourself during the speaking test.

TEST 3

Part 1 *Time for this part: 3 min.*

INTERVIEW

What do you have to do in Part 1 of Paper 5?

Do

... show interest in what other people say.

Don't

... interrupt the other candidate.

HELP

How can you correct yourself if you know you have made an error?

Group Work Activity

Work in groups of three.
One of you will be the *Interlocutor*, and the other two will be the *Candidates.*

INTERLOCUTOR
Prepare some questions for your candidates about what they did on holiday last year.
- what they did
- what they would have liked to do
- whether they would like to go to the same place again

CANDIDATES
Look at the Dos and Don'ts on the left and think about your answers.
Where would you like to go on holiday this year?

Carry out the interview.

Where did you go last summer?
Was it fun?
Would you go there again?
Where would you rather have gone?
Where will you go this year?

EASY   DIFFICULT
1 2 3 4 5 | *How difficult was this part?*

CANDIDATE A   Part 2 *Time for this part:* 4 min.

Pair Work Activity

ON YOUR OWN
Look at the two pictures.
How are they similar?
How are they different?
Who do you think built these places?
Why do you think they were built?
What kind of society do they represent?

WITH A PARTNER
Candidate A:
Compare and contrast your pictures for your partner.
Candidate B:
Respond to your partner's ideas.

Which place would you like to visit?

**INDIVIDUAL
LONG
TURN**

What do you have to do in Part 2 of Paper 5?

 Do

... give your personal reaction to the pictures – how do they make you feel?

 **Don't**

... worry if you haven't seen the places before – use your imagination.

 **Help**

How many ways do you know of giving reasons for your decisions.

one shows a state-of-the-art high-rise building, representing the modern world
the other shows a prehistoric monument representing sacred rites and ritual

TEST 4

TOTAL TIME
15 MIN.

Part 2 *Time for this part:* 4 MIN.

CANDIDATE B

**INDIVIDUAL
LONG
TURN**

What do you have to do in Part 2 of Paper 5?

**Do**

... give your personal reaction to the pictures - how do they make you feel?

**Don't**

... worry if you haven't seen the places before - use your imagination.

![Help icon]**Help**

How many ways do you know of giving reasons for your decisions.

Pair Work Activity

ON YOUR OWN
Look at the two pictures.
How are they similar?
How are they different?
Who do you think might visit these places?
Why do you think someone would visit these places?

WITH A PARTNER
Candidate A:
Compare and contrast your pictures for your partner.
Candidate B:
Respond to your partner's ideas.

Which place would you like to visit?

one shows a Japanese water garden, a place for quiet reflection
the other shows a beach filled with sunbeds, a place for relaxation and companionship

EASY | DIFFICULT
1 2 3 4 5 | *How difficult was this part?*

Part 3 *Time for this part:* 3 MIN.

TOTAL TIME
15 MIN.

Group Work Activity

CANDIDATES
You are members of the city council and you need to take some steps to reduce pollution. Below are some suggestions.

You don't have to agree. Discuss your plans for three minutes.

INTERLOCUTOR
Listen to the candidates and use the evaluation sheet to grade them. Tell the candidates how well they did and where they need improvement.

COLLABORATIVE TASK

What do you have to do in Part 3 of Paper 5?

✓ *Do*

... speak and encourage your partner to give his/her views.

💣 *Don't*

... forget to give reasons for your opinions.

 *HELP*

How can you summarise the discussion?

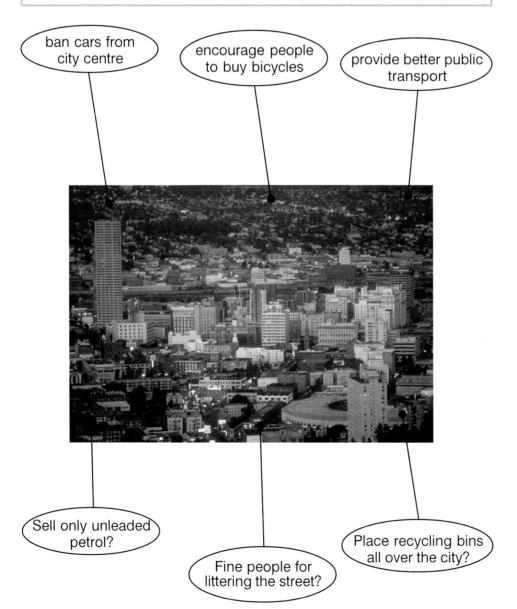

(ban cars from city centre)

(encourage people to buy bicycles)

(provide better public transport)

(Sell only unleaded petrol?)

(Fine people for littering the street?)

(Place recycling bins all over the city?)

TEST 4

How difficult was this part? EASY DIFFICULT 1 2 3 4 5

Part 4 *Time for this part:* 4 min.

THREE - WAY DISCUSSION

What do you have to do in Part 4 of Paper 5?

**Do**

... think about what you have heard on the news and read in newspapers.

**Don't**

... worry about agreeing with the other candidate(s).

HELP

How can you check that you are being understood?

Group Work Activity

1) Work alone.
Think of three ways in which you as an individual can help to protect the environment.
Here are some suggestions. You can add any of your own.

• Switch off all electrical appliances (TV, radio, lights) when they are not being used.

• Never throw papers, cans and wrappers in the street.

• Never throw rubbish into the sea.

• Ask shop assistants to give you paper bags instead of plastic ones.

2) Work in groups of three.

Discuss your ideas.

• Do you think they are all practical?

• Which ones are the easiest to apply?

• Which ones do you always do?

• Which ones do you never do?

• Can you agree on the single most important one?

TOTAL TIME
15 MIN.

PERSONAL PROGRESS RECORD

Speaking Test Four
Personal Progress Record

I feel good about:

I need to practise:

USEFUL HINTS

☀ Ways to give reasons for decisions:

> I think...
> I believe...
> I am sure/certain of this because...

☀ Ways to ensure your listener understands you:

> Do you see what I mean?
> Do you understand?
> Is that clear?

Use this record to keep notes on the following:

1. The aspects of the speaking test that you feel confident with.

2. The aspects of the speaking test that you feel you need to work on.

3. Useful language items that you can use to help yourself during the speaking test.

TEST 4

TOTAL TIME
15 min.

Part 1 *Time for this part:* 3 min.

INTERVIEW

What do you have to do in Part 1 of Paper 5?

Do

... think about your answers and any personal experience you have.

Don't

... worry if you forget a word.

👤 HELP

What ways do you know of asking someone to repeat what they said?

Group Work Activity

1) Work alone.
What is important to you in your friendships? Put the ideas below into the columns according to your opinion. Add other characteristics you think might be important.

> ## Give REASONS FOR YOUR IDEAS!
> ### Friends
>
> | | |
> |---|---|
> | rich | amusing |
> | good looking | listen to my problems |
> | share same interests | same age as me |
> | wear nice clothes | Other? |
>
> **Important:**
> ....
> ....
> ....
> ....
> ....
> because:
> ....
> ....
> ....
> ....
>
> **Not important:**
> ....
> ....
> ....
> ....
> ....
> because:
> ....
> ....
> ....
> ....

2) Work in groups of three.
One of you will be the **Interlocutor** and the other two will be the **Candidates.**

INTERLOCUTOR
Prepare some questions for the candidates based on the ideas above.

CANDIDATES
What questions do you think you might be asked? Think about your answers.

Carry out the interview.

Is it important that your friends are rich?
Are all your friends the same age as you?
What is the most important aspect in a friendship?

EASY   DIFFICULT
1 2 3 4 5 | *How difficult was this part?*

CANDIDATE A   Part 2 *Time for this part:* 4 MIN.

Group Work Activity

INTERLOCUTOR
Listen to the candidate. After about one minute, stop the candidate who is speaking and ask the other candidate to comment briefly (about 20 seconds) on the photographs.

Candidate A:
Speak alone.

Candidate B:
Listen to what the other candidate says and comment when asked.

How do the pictures make you feel?

both seem lonely
in one, the man looks unemployed, poor and hungry
in the other, the man may be retired, and alone

INDIVIDUAL LONG TURN

What do you have to do in Part 2 of Paper 5?

✔ **Do**

... say how the photos make you feel.

● **Don't**

... ask the other candidate to speak at this point.

🧑‍🦯 **Help**

Think about the instructions:
compare and contrast.
How is this different from *describe*?

TEST 5

How difficult was this part? EASY 1 2 3 4 5 DIFFICULT

TOTAL TIME
15 MIN.

Part 2 *Time for this part:* 4 MIN.   **CANDIDATE B**

INDIVIDUAL LONG TURN

What do you have to do in Part 2 of Paper 5?

Do

... say how the photos make you feel.

Don't

... ask the other candidate to speak at this point.

Help

Think about the instructions:
compare and contrast.
How is this different from *describe*?

both are rural scenes
one shows bales of hay
the other shows a dutch
windmill

Group Work Activity

INTERLOCUTOR
Listen to the candidate. After about one minute, stop the candidate who is speaking and ask the other candidate to comment briefly (about 20 seconds) on the photographs.

Candidate A:
Listen to what the other candidate says and comment when asked.

Candidate B:
Speak alone.

Would you like to live in the country?

EASY   DIFFICULT
1 2 3 4 5   *How difficult was this part?*

Part 3 *Time for this part:* 3 MIN.

Group Work Activity

CANDIDATES
There is a long weekend coming up next week.
How would you like to spend it?

You don't have to agree. Discuss your ideas for three minutes.

Here are some possibilities:

- swimming, scuba diving, sunbathing
- camping, hiking, mountain climbing
- games, cinema restaurants

INTERLOCUTORS
Listen to the candidates and use the evaluation sheet to grade them. Tell the candidates how well they did, and where they need improvement.

COLLABORATIVE TASK

What do you have to do in Part 3 of Paper 5?

✓ *Do*

... allow other people their chance to speak.

Don't

... allow long pauses to come into the conversation

*HELP*

How can you encourage a shy candidate to enter into the conversation?

How difficult was this part? | EASY DIFFICULT | 1 2 3 4 5

TOTAL TIME
15 min.

Part 4 *Time for this part:* 4 min.

THREE- WAY DISCUSSION

What do you have to do in Part 4 of Paper 5?

Do

... feel free to raise topics of your own if you think they are relevant.

Don't

... raise topics that have no connection with the discussion.

HELP

Think of some ways of suggesting a topic for discussion.

Group Work Activity

Work in groups of three.

In part four of the test, the Interlocutor will begin a discussion with you using issues that have been raised in part three.

Look at part three. What themes were raised?
Make a list of FIVE questions that you think the Interlocutor might raise in part four.

Pass your questions to another group.

Discuss the questions that the other group has given you. Can you all decide on one answer?

Distance
Advantages and disadvantages of different places
Active or relaxed?
Sports or culture?
Season?

EASY   DIFFICULT
1 2 3 4 5   *How difficult was this part?*

Speaking Test Five
Personal Progress Record

I feel good about:

I need to practise:

USEFUL HINTS

✳ Ways to ask for repetition:

Sorry, what did you say?
Could you repeat that, please?
Can you say that again, please?

✳ Ways to suggest a topic for discussion:

Have you thought about...
I'd like to suggest ...
Can I point out...

**PERSONAL
PROGRESS
RECORD**

Use this record to keep notes on the following:

1. The aspects of the speaking test that you feel confident with.

2. The aspects of the speaking test that you feel you need to work on.

3. Useful language items that you can use to help yourself during the speaking test.

TEST 5

Candidate Name: _____

Candidate Signature: _____

Use a pencil

For Parts 1, 3 and 4:
Mark ONE letter for each question.

For example if you think **B** is the right answer to the question, mark your answer sheet like this:

0	A	B	C

For Part 2:
Write your answers in the spaces next to the numbers like this:

0	example

Part 1

1	A	B	C
2	A	B	C
3	A	B	C
4	A	B	C
5	A	B	C
6	A	B	C
7	A	B	C
8	A	B	C

Part 2

Do not write here

9		
10		
11		
12		
13		
14		
15		
16		
17		
18		

Part 4

24	T	F
25	T	F
26	T	F
27	T	F
28	T	F
29	T	F
30	T	F

Part 3

19	A	B	C	D	E	F
20	A	B	C	D	E	F
21	A	B	C	D	E	F
22	A	B	C	D	E	F
23	A	B	C	D	E	F

Listening Test 2
Candidate Answer Sheet

Candidate Name: _____

Candidate Signature: _____

Use a pencil

For Parts 1, 3 and 4:
Mark ONE letter for each question.

For example if you think **B** is the right answer to the question, mark your answer sheet like this:

0	A	B	C
	☐	■	☐

For Part 2:
Write your answers in the spaces next to the numbers like this:

0	example

Part 1

1	A ☐	B ☐	C ☐
2	A ☐	B ☐	C ☐
3	A ☐	B ☐	C ☐
4	A ☐	B ☐	C ☐
5	A ☐	B ☐	C ☐
6	A ☐	B ☐	C ☐
7	A ☐	B ☐	C ☐
8	A ☐	B ☐	C ☐

Part 2

		Do not write here
9		☐ ☐
10		☐ ☐
11		☐ ☐
12		☐ ☐
13		☐ ☐
14		☐ ☐
15		☐ ☐
16		☐ ☐
17		☐ ☐
18		☐ ☐

Part 3

19	A ☐	B ☐	C ☐	D ☐	E ☐	F ☐
20	A ☐	B ☐	C ☐	D ☐	E ☐	F ☐
21	A ☐	B ☐	C ☐	D ☐	E ☐	F ☐
22	A ☐	B ☐	C ☐	D ☐	E ☐	F ☐
23	A ☐	B ☐	C ☐	D ☐	E ☐	F ☐

Part 4

24	T ☐	F ☐
25	T ☐	F ☐
26	T ☐	F ☐
27	T ☐	F ☐
28	T ☐	F ☐
29	T ☐	F ☐
30	T ☐	F ☐

Candidate Name: _____

Candidate Signature: _____

Use a pencil

For Parts 1, 3 and 4:
Mark ONE letter for each question.

For example if you think **B** is the right answer to the question, mark your answer sheet like this:

0	A	B	C
	☐	■	☐

For Part 2:
Write your answers in the spaces next to the numbers like this:

0	example

Part 1

	A	B	C
1	☐	☐	☐
2	☐	☐	☐
3	☐	☐	☐
4	☐	☐	☐
5	☐	☐	☐
6	☐	☐	☐
7	☐	☐	☐
8	☐	☐	☐

Part 2

		Do not write here
9		☐ ☐
10		☐ ☐
11		☐ ☐
12		☐ ☐
13		☐ ☐
14		☐ ☐
15		☐ ☐
16		☐ ☐
17		☐ ☐
18		☐ ☐

Part 3

	A	B	C	D	E	F
19	☐	☐	☐	☐	☐	☐
20	☐	☐	☐	☐	☐	☐
21	☐	☐	☐	☐	☐	☐
22	☐	☐	☐	☐	☐	☐
23	☐	☐	☐	☐	☐	☐

Part 4

	Y	N
24	☐	☐
25	☐	☐
26	☐	☐
27	☐	☐
28	☐	☐
29	☐	☐
30	☐	☐

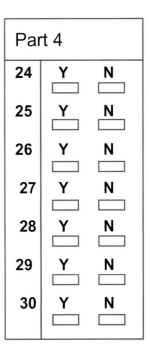

Candidate Name: _____

Candidate Signature: _____

Use a pencil

For Parts 1, 3 and 4:
Mark ONE letter for each question.

For example if you think **B** is the right answer to the question, mark your answer sheet like this:

0	A	B	C
	☐	■	☐

For Part 2:
Write your answers in the spaces next to the numbers like this:

0	example

Part 1

	A	B	C
1	☐	☐	☐
2	☐	☐	☐
3	☐	☐	☐
4	☐	☐	☐
5	☐	☐	☐
6	☐	☐	☐
7	☐	☐	☐
8	☐	☐	☐

Part 2

		Do not write here
9		☐ ☐
10		☐ ☐
11		☐ ☐
12		☐ ☐
13		☐ ☐
14		☐ ☐
15		☐ ☐
16		☐ ☐
17		☐ ☐
18		☐ ☐

Part 3

	A	B	C	D	E	F
19	☐	☐	☐	☐	☐	☐
20	☐	☐	☐	☐	☐	☐
21	☐	☐	☐	☐	☐	☐
22	☐	☐	☐	☐	☐	☐
23	☐	☐	☐	☐	☐	☐

Part 4

	A	B	C
24	☐	☐	☐
25	☐	☐	☐
26	☐	☐	☐
27	☐	☐	☐
28	☐	☐	☐
29	☐	☐	☐
30	☐	☐	☐

Listening Test 5
Candidate Answer Sheet

Candidate Name: _____

Candidate Signature: _____

Use a pencil

For Parts 1, 3 and 4:
Mark ONE letter for each question.

For example if you think **B** is the right answer to the question, mark your answer sheet like this:

0	A	B	C
	☐	■	☐

For Parts 2:
Write your answers in the spaces next to the numbers like this:

0	example

Part 1

	A	B	C
1	☐	☐	☐
2	☐	☐	☐
3	☐	☐	☐
4	☐	☐	☐
5	☐	☐	☐
6	☐	☐	☐
7	☐	☐	☐
8	☐	☐	☐

Part 2

Do not write here

9		☐ ☐
10		☐ ☐
11		☐ ☐
12		☐ ☐
13		☐ ☐
14		☐ ☐
15		☐ ☐
16		☐ ☐
17		☐ ☐
18		☐ ☐

Part 3

	A	B	C	D	E	F
19	☐	☐	☐	☐	☐	☐
20	☐	☐	☐	☐	☐	☐
21	☐	☐	☐	☐	☐	☐
22	☐	☐	☐	☐	☐	☐
23	☐	☐	☐	☐	☐	☐

Part 4

	P	J	N
24	☐	☐	☐
25	☐	☐	☐
26	☐	☐	☐
27	☐	☐	☐
28	☐	☐	☐
29	☐	☐	☐
30	☐	☐	☐

Candidate Name: _____

(Circle one number for each area tested)

Grammar and Vocabulary

| 1 | 2 | 3 | 4 | 5 | G & V |

Assessment of the candidate's use of grammar items and the appropriate use and range of vocabulary without continually halting to search for a word or to think about how to construct a grammatical sentence.

Discourse Management

| 1 | 2 | 3 | 4 | 5 | DM |

Evaluation of the candidate's ability to use an appropriate range of linguistic resources to organise sentences, express opinions and/or justify a point of view while maintaining a coherent flow of speech.

Pronunciation

| 1 | 2 | 3 | 4 | 5 | P |

Assessment of the candidate's ability to produce correct individual sounds, word and sentence stress, and proper intonation to convey meaning.

Interactive Communication

| 1 | 2 | 3 | 4 | 5 | IC |

Evaluation of the candidate's ability to initiate and respond appropriately according to the task, taking turns in the discussion and contributing to the development of the task.

Global Achievement

| 1 | 2 | 3 | 4 | 5 | GA |

An overall assessment of the candidate's ability to tackle the four separate tasks at hand.

Candidate Name: _____

(Circle one number for each area tested)

Grammar and Vocabulary

1	2	3	4	5	G & V

Assessment of the candidate's use of grammar items and the appropriate use and range of vocabulary without continually halting to search for a word or to think about how to construct a grammatical sentence.

Discourse Management

1	2	3	4	5	DM

Evaluation of the candidate's ability to use an appropriate range of linguistic resources to organise sentences, express opinions and/or justify a point of view while maintaining a coherent flow of speech.

Pronunciation

1	2	3	4	5	P

Assessment of the candidate's ability to produce correct individual sounds, word and sentence stress, and proper intonation to convey meaning.

Interactive Communication

1	2	3	4	5	IC

Evaluation of the candidate's ability to initiate and respond appropriately according to the task, taking turns in the discussion and contributing to the development of the task.

Global Achievement

1	2	3	4	5	GA

An overall assessment of the candidate's ability to tackle the four separate tasks at hand.

Candidate Name: _____

(Circle one number for each area tested)

Grammar and Vocabulary

| 1 | 2 | 3 | 4 | 5 | G & V |

Assessment of the candidate's use of grammar items and the appropriate use and range of vocabulary without continually halting to search for a word or to think about how to construct a grammatical sentence.

Discourse Management

| 1 | 2 | 3 | 4 | 5 | DM |

Evaluation of the candidate's ability to use an appropriate range of linguistic resources to organise sentences, express opinions and/or justify a point of view while maintaining a coherent flow of speech.

Pronunciation

| 1 | 2 | 3 | 4 | 5 | P |

Assessment of the candidate's ability to produce correct individual sounds, word and sentence stress, and proper intonation to convey meaning.

Interactive Communication

| 1 | 2 | 3 | 4 | 5 | IC |

Evaluation of the candidate's ability to initiate and respond appropriately according to the task, taking turns in the discussion and contributing to the development of the task.

Global Achievement

| 1 | 2 | 3 | 4 | 5 | GA |

An overall assessment of the candidate's ability to tackle the four separate tasks at hand.

Candidate Name: _____

(Circle one number for each area tested)

Grammar and Vocabulary

| 1 | 2 | 3 | 4 | 5 | G & V |

Assessment of the candidate's use of grammar items and the appropriate use and range of vocabulary without continually halting to search for a word or to think about how to construct a grammatical sentence.

Discourse Management

| 1 | 2 | 3 | 4 | 5 | DM |

Evaluation of the candidate's ability to use an appropriate range of linguistic resources to organise sentences, express opinions and/or justify a point of view while maintaining a coherent flow of speech.

Pronunciation

| 1 | 2 | 3 | 4 | 5 | P |

Assessment of the candidate's ability to produce correct individual sounds, word and sentence stress, and proper intonation to convey meaning.

Interactive Communication

| 1 | 2 | 3 | 4 | 5 | IC |

Evaluation of the candidate's ability to initiate and respond appropriately according to the task, taking turns in the discussion and contributing to the development of the task.

Global Achievement

| 1 | 2 | 3 | 4 | 5 | GA |

An overall assessment of the candidate's ability to tackle the four separate tasks at hand.

Candidate Name: _____

(Circle one number for each area tested)

Grammar and Vocabulary

| 1 | 2 | 3 | 4 | 5 | G & V |

Assessment of the candidate's use of grammar items and the appropriate use and range of vocabulary without continually halting to search for a word or to think about how to construct a grammatical sentence.

Discourse Management

| 1 | 2 | 3 | 4 | 5 | DM |

Evaluation of the candidate's ability to use an appropriate range of linguistic resources to organise sentences, express opinions and/or justify a point of view while maintaining a coherent flow of speech.

Pronunciation

| 1 | 2 | 3 | 4 | 5 | P |

Assessment of the candidate's ability to produce correct individual sounds, word and sentence stress, and proper intonation to convey meaning.

Interactive Communication

| 1 | 2 | 3 | 4 | 5 | IC |

Evaluation of the candidate's ability to initiate and respond appropriately according to the task, taking turns in the discussion and contributing to the development of the task.

Global Achievement

| 1 | 2 | 3 | 4 | 5 | GA |

An overall assessment of the candidate's ability to tackle the four separate tasks at hand.

Part 1

Question 1

Do you know what I found out today? You know Mary? She's teaching forty two hours a week... yeah, you heard right... and she's got a small son - it would drive me mad... I don't know how she does it with a husband who won't do a hand's turn in the house... I mean she'll have all the housework to do on top of the essays and reading for the course... Anyway, we'll have to be more flexible with assignment deadlines in her case, but don't let it get around. I don't want everybody hearing about it and then handing work in late and giving us heart-breaking stories about how much they have to do outside course hours, you know - OK?

Question 2

Well how do you get it going, then? I've put the stuff in the drum and the powder in the drawer, set the temperature... but it won't go. So how do you get the thing working? What button? There's a sign on one of the buttons on the top, looks like a snail, sort of a curly wurly thing, is that it? Whoops, yes, that's the one, it's going now. Will it stop by itself? Fully automatic... that's amazing. Well thank you very much, that's lovely.

Question 3

A: Do you sell woks?
B: What?
A: Woks.
B: What's that then?
A: It's a kind of Chinese frying pan.
B: Nah... glasses and plates and that, but no whacks.
  What did you call it again?
A: A wok.
B: Hang about, what's this?
A: That's an omelette pan.
B: Won't it do you?
A: No, I said I wanted a Chinese frying pan... a wok.
B: Doesn't look like we've got what you're after, then, eh?
A: Forget it.

Question 4

Does anybody else want to order anything? I'm about to call Vesuvio's for some pizzas and stuff... What? I don't think they do pizzas with no cheese on them. They do? What do you call them? OK, one of those... sorry? ... It's a restaurant, so it's got plenty of different dishes... yeah, there are salads as well if anybody fancies one... With red beans and lettuce? I'm not keen myself, it's a bit heavy going but get one if you like. There are six of us, it'll get eaten. Now, listen, if everyone wants a pizza each, we're going to end up with pizza overkill. Can't we order one pizza between two of us? I wish I'd never suggested the idea now.

Question 5

I don't know what on Earth's wrong - every morning when I get up I have this really bad stomach ache and a pain in my back. When I get up and start moving around it goes away and as the rest of the day goes on I forget all about it. Then the following morning there it is again, and I feel lousy for about a quarter of an hour or so. You don't feel like bothering the doctor for something so... you know, probably trivial, do you?... With some of them being so busy and all... Then again while it lasts, it really isn't that trivial, it's quite severe. I don't know... What should I do about it?

Question 6

How are you getting on with the assignment? I don't know where to begin. To tell you the truth, I've never had to write anything this long and detailed before. They gave us a list of books to read - are we supposed to read ALL of them? Where do you find the time for that? I don't know... do you read just BITS of the books? Do you read just one chapter of each, and if so, how do you know which chapter's the most important one? I'm lost, to be honest. Shall I phone Jill? She got a good mark for HER last assignment, maybe I can pick her brains and she can enlighten us both... yeah, I'll do that... Bye!

Question 7

Who is it? Who? I'm sorry, you're supposed to ring the bell of the person you want to visit... It's three in the morning, why are you disturbing me? Your what?... Your cat's in the entrance hall and you can't open the outside door? Do me a favour... do you think I'm that stupid? How did it get into a block of flats not its own in the first place? Go away before I call the police. There's too many strange people trying to break into flats these days. Well, you certainly sound like a strange person to me. If there's really a cat, then it won't come to any harm before morning, so come back when it's daylight.

Question 8
Somebody rang my bell at three in the morning pretending his cat was in the entrance hall and he couldn't get her out. I thought, have you ever heard anything like the cheek of it, I told him to get lost or I'd call the police. He got quite irate, and was quite insistent. You want to be careful, I said, there's a lot of it about and they're cracking down. Anyway... I came down this morning and there's this little tortoiseshell sitting on the hall table meowing at me, and a gentleman turns up and says through the glass door, that's my cat, she got in there last night and some nasty old witch refused to open the door for me. I had a good laugh at that, I felt sorry for him then, of course, but I still think you can't be too careful.

Part 2

Host: This week we have with us Chini Jon, who is manager of the Dynasty, one of the most successful Chinese restaurants in the city. The British have long had a great passion for Chinese food. Chini, why do you think that is?
Guest: I don't know - I often think that it's because British food used to be so bland! ... boring actually! That's why Chinese and Indian food became so very popular here.
Host: How does British Chinese food compare with the real Chinese food in Taiwan, where you were born?
Guest: Well, to be quite honest, thirty years ago when I first came to this country, the so-called Chinese food here bore no resemblance to the food back home: we cook most things for a very short time over a very high heat... so that the vegetables stay crisp and colourful, but here they cooked things for ages and it went all
soft and mushy. We use a lot of garlic and ginger and hot chillies, and the British were very wary of these things, so the food they wanted and demanded actually had very little taste. Also, most people seemed to think of Chinese restaurants as cheap - somewhere you went when you couldn't afford anything better, and so they wouldn't pay for good quality even if you were offering it.
Host: But have things changed for the better?
Guest: Oh, very much so! It's a fact that the British have become much more interested in food than they used to be - the old cliche about bad British food isn't true any more. People are more adventurous and more demanding. They have travelled more widely and they are much more knowledgeable than they were. The Dynasty isn't a cheap place, as you know, David, but...
Host: The food is fabulous.
Guest: Well, thanks, but I do know that! What I was going to say is that it isn't cheap but it *is* very successful. People are realising now that there is a lot more to Chinese food than just the old sweet and sour pork and Peking duck... And also... that if you want quality you have to be prepared to pay for it. We have some great seafood and some excellent vegetarian cooking to offer as well as the old favourites.
Host: Now, my old favourite is Chop Suey...
Guest: Well, you'll have to go somewhere else!
Host: Now why is that?
Guest: Chop Suey isn't a real Chinese dish - the Americans invented it!
Host: Another illusion shattered! ...The Dynasty is open from eight o'clock in the evening until late, and you can find it at number 54, Princess Alexandra Walk - and remember...... book well in advance!

Part 3

Speaker One
It was the first time I had been away from home. I went to France to work as an assistant English teacher in a school there. I was what... eighteen. I didn't know how to cook, I had never had to wash my own clothes, I didn't know how to handle money, and I had never really had much of a social life with people my own age. It was a recipe for disaster, really, but I was so innocent I never thought about the possible problems and I suppose in a way my innocence got me through.

Speaker Two
I must have been eleven years old. My parents sent me to a boarding school and the idea was to make you learn independence from an early age. I don't think it's a good idea, really... OK, you learn independence for sure, but it made me really arrogant and opinionated for a long period of my life... leaving boarding school and getting a job in the real world was very good for me, I think.

Speaker Three
I was eight. Yeah... eight. I just packed a bag with some biscuits and a pair of clean socks and left. We lived in the country and there wasn't another house for miles, but I found one. I remember telling the old farmer who answered the door that I had left home and needed a job. I assured him I had no plans to get married and wouldn't be leaving in a hurry. He asked me who my parents were and went and phoned them... my father turned up in the car an hour

later and took me home. I was furious... Just one day of freedom!

Speaker Four

I didn't leave home until I was thirty five. Friends used to laugh at me, even pity me, I think, but I don't see what the big deal is. I had a good job, I had my own car, my own room and bathroom... and, I think in many ways, I had a lot more freedom to do my own thing than many of my friends who were paying mortgages and rent. Eventually I had to leave because I was transferred with my job to another city, but I still go back home whenever I can.

Speaker Five

I don't know if you can call it leaving home or not - I moved out at twenty three, not too far away, and my mother virtually moved in with me... she was forever round, cleaning and cooking for me as though I were totally helpless... The freezer was bursting with the stuff she kept cooking for me... every so often I had to throw it all out and pretend it was delicious... I kept telling her, "Look, I know how to use the washing machine, I'm a pretty good cook," - which she isn't, by the way - and I did everything short of actually telling her to go away and leave me to get on with things in my own way.

Part 4

A: Can I help you?
B: Yes, I'm looking for a book.
A: Do you have the title?
B: Yes, it's 'Colloquial Mexican' by Juan Xavier.
A: Hmmm, I don't think we..
B: Oh, don't tell me you don't have it in stock either! You were my last hope!
A: Well, let me just check... if we don't have it in stock we can always order it for you.
B: I've been to every bookshop in town!
A: I suppose it's a bit of an unusual book, really.
B: You've got books for learning some fairly uncommon languages - Basque, Icelandic, Swahili...
A: Yes, but I can't see the one you want, what was it again?
B: Mexican.
A: Mmmm, not very much in demand, Mexican...
B: Well possibly, but I do need it. I'm going there on business and they recommended that I learn a bit, you see...
A: I see, mmm now let me look ... Oh, I think I've found it ... No, sorry that's a Hungarian one. Well, that's fairly obscure too, isn't it?
B: But unlikely to be of much help in Mexico, I would have thought.
A: Now what's this here? I'll just blow the dust off it, (blows) and it's...
B: That's the one! Well it seems my luck has changed after all.
A: Ooh, it isn't especially cheap, though and it seems ....
B: No problem, it's the only one in town. I'll take it.
A: Fine, fine, I was just going to offer you a small discount as the cover is a bit torn ...
B: Well possibly, but I do need it. I'm going there on business and they recommended me to learn a bit, you know.
A: I see, mmm now let me look ... Oh I think I found it ... No, sorry that's a Hungarian one. Well, that's fairly obscure too, isn't it?
B: But unlikely to be of much help in Albania, I would have thought.
A: Now what's this here? I'll just blow the dust off it, (blows) and it's...
B: That's the one! Well it seems my luck has changed after all.
A: Ooh, it isn't especially cheap, though and it seems ....
B: No problem, it's the only one in town. I'll take it.
A: Fine, fine, I was just going to offer you a small discount as the cover is a bit torn ...

Part 1

Question 1

Ok, fine, if that's the way you feel, I'll change it... but remember this took ages to make... if you're going to raise objections to all of them, we'll never get this exhibition ready on time... I know you care about the quality of the work but we also need to think about the money we intend to make out of this, so if you want some money as well, you'll have to learn to make a few compromises, that's all.

Question 2

... and now the moment we've all been waiting for, the prize awards. In order to qualify for the big prize... a luxury car, Ed needed at least 1,000 points, but only gained 950 points... hard luck Ed, you came pretty close though... Let's have a look at it anyway... lovely, isn't it, fully automatic... and remember it can be yours ... all you need to do is collect 1,000 points or more. Still, Ed will not leave empty-handed ... this is for you Ed ... it's also automatic, though it doesn't run as fast... sorry? ... yes Ed, any type of coffee .. mmm? yes, cappuccino too...

Question 3

I was having lunch with my father in a small restaurant on the side of a hill, overlooking the sea when suddenly... a fighter plane comes roaring practically over our heads .. well or so it seemed to us ... the noise was deafening ... and then it starts descending, almost following the hill's contour ... and then seconds later it crashes into the sea ... causing huge waves which came up as high as the restaurant ... splashing everybody .. . and then the captain asked all the passengers to go inside as the sea was getting too rough ... ermmm... yes... somehow we were on a ship, one of those huge transatlantic cruisers .... and the captain was my father .... weird ... well, that's all I remember....

Question 4

He rang me the other night from Sweden and said, can you put me up at your place for a week next month? I said, well look, this place is really very small; I haven't got room. If I've moved... 'cos I am thinking of doing, and found somewhere bigger by next month, you know, then yes, it'll be ok, I suppose, I didn't really know what else to say, you can't just sort of say no, directly... Anyway, he's gone and bought his ticket! I'll have to sleep on the floor, I suppose.

Question 5

Oh, him... he's never wrong. Thinks everybody else is foolish and the only way is his way. There's loads of people like that... makes it a lot worse when you're supposed to be teaching one. It happens to be one of my pet hates - people who obviously know absolutely nothing about a subject but who nevertheless *insist* on giving you their opinion loud and clear. Of course... you have to put on that nonsense about "that's certainly a point, but have you considered...?" and all that. It was all I could do to stop myself from yelling this morning, though.

Question 6

Hello? Hi, mum, it's me... look, don't worry, but I'm in hospital - yes, in, not at... look, I'm OK, I just had a bit of an accident... in the car yes.. I'm fine, really... well, ... they're not so sure, so I have to stay in a day or two. They'll get it seen to though, so i thought I had just better let you know, OK?... No, I feel fine... as good as can be expected, a bit shaken up, that's all. Yes... well some soap, if you can, toothpaste and stuff, a few books and my Walkman... some cassettes. No, really, I'm OK. They're being really nice, no... no carnations, you don't need - Ok, ok, some grapes if you want, but really it's soap and deodorant... more that type of thing. Don't sound so worried, really...

Question 7

Man: ... no really I'd still be running about if it wasn't for you.

Woman: Come on, it wasn't as if you had loads of stuff... and it was practically down the street.

Man: Well ok, but I still needed your car, I couldn't just carry them over myself...

Woman: Still, you did do all the packing yourself.

Man: True, but this place would look like a jumble sale if you hadn't helped.

Woman: Not much to sell, is there?

Man: Anyway... I'd still like to buy you dinner.

Woman: All right, but nothing fancy.

Man: Great, what about Vittorio's, tomorrow at six?

Question 8

Hello? I beg your pardon? No... No, I'm afraid not. Courtesy Cars? - Yes, people often get the numbers conf... no, it **isn't**, madam, it's a private house... I'm not running any sort of service! Look... it's a bad line, you had better ring off... I don't know what their number is. I'm not directory enquiries either... Can I what? NO, I can't, not even if I wanted to. How can I put you through to Courtesy Cars? I'm not an operator **either**. Look I'm going to hang up now, OK?

Part 2

Good evening everyone. I am delighted to welcome you to the launch of our 'New English Dictionary'. This is a particularly exciting occasion for us here at Heritage Press. We believe our dictionary will be a landmark in the history of the English language. We predict that it will form part of the linguistic heritage passed on to future generations.

What we are offering is a 'NEW' English Dictionary. I emphasize the word 'new' deliberately. In addition to presenting a whole new concept in terms of language reference, our new dictionary focuses on the changing nature of the English language.

First, let me tell you about our new concept. We use clear, jargon-free English to ensure exceptional clarity. A defining vocabulary of 3,000 words guarantees instant understanding of language, and our revolutionary page design offers quick and easy access to all areas.

Second, let me explain a little about the actual nature of the entries. As a result of our extensive language research, we have included thousands of new words and meanings, monitored by our exceptional linguistics staff. The information we provide is up to the minute, a very important feature in our fast changing world. I only need to mention such fields as Science and Technology, International English and Slang, for you to appreciate why this is necessary. To improve your command of the language, we have included information on recent changes in usage as well. Our guide to pronunciation shows the most important changes to the English language which have taken place in the twentieth century. These areas will help you to speak, read and write with confidence and authority.

I have only mentioned the key features of Heritage Press's 'New English Dictionary'. As our time is almost up, I would like to invite you to stay and mingle with our researchers, writers and editors at the buffet supper in the adjoining room. They will be pleased to answer any questions you may have and also to discuss the additional features.

Remember, here at 'Heritage Press' we respect our language heritage, building on the past and preparing for the future.

Enjoy your evening.

Part 3

Speaker 1

I'm a traditionalist myself. I think Shakespeare should be performed in seventeenth century costume and done with music from the same period. This performance to me was a mess - they were trying to be modern and original and it just ended up being totally confusing. I really have no idea what point the director was trying to make. I wonder if he had either.

Speaker 2

I don't know what I think really... know what I mean? I mean, I'm not up on Shakespeare really... I haven't been to a play like this before. I thought they'd all be dressed up like what's his name... *Hamlet*. But they weren't. They had all sort of spears and monkey fur round their heads. Dead weird. I don't know if I enjoyed it or not. Cost a fair bit for the ticket, mind.

Speaker 3

A very interesting concept. I was involved, yes, definitely... I don't think it has been done this way up to now. Shakespeare in African tribal costume isn't new, of course... I've seen *Macbeth* done by an African company this way before, but never *Much Ado About Nothing*. No, to be honest I haven't a clue WHY they did it this way, but I thought the costumes were nice, didn't you?

Speaker 4

It was a total waste of the audience's time and money. After the interval we decided we'd just stay in the bar. There could have been good, valid artistic reasons for performing *Much Ado* in Zulu costume but this production had none - it was done just for the sake of novelty, and it got very silly. They'll be performing *Hamlet* on roller skates or *Julius Caesar* under water next.

Speaker 5

We've seen Shakespeare in sixteenth century costume, nineteenth century costume, twentieth century costume, modern dress... just about any kind of costume you can think of. It's all been done before - so why not do *Much Ado* in Zulu costume? It made a change, that's all that mattered. Most people have seen this play so often I don't think they'd really care if they did it standing on their heads or dressed as teddy bears. Wouldn't break my heart if they never do *Much Ado* again, to be honest.

Woman: Hello dear...

Man: Evening.

Woman: Oh, no - another cheerful evening ahead of us, I see.

Man: Oh, don't start, I've had a bad enough day as it is. Do you want me to tell you about it?

Woman: Well, I dare say you're going to anyway. Do you want to ask me about my day, for a change?

Man: We lost the Avalon contract, the mineral water...

Woman: I thought not.

Man: You know, they said they didn't like ANY of my advertising ideas and so...

Woman: What's Avalon?

Man: The mineral water company! I just told you.

Woman: I wasn't really listening.

Man: It was brilliant! Fantastic adverts we'd designed, and they decide we're no good! Makes my blood boil... We spent weeks and weeks on it... so I've got the sack. I said I've got the sack.

Woman: Yes, I heard.

Man: And?

Woman: I don't know! What do you want me to do about it?

Man: What about the villa in the South of France?

Woman: Sell it.

Man: And the Alfa Romeo?

Woman: Sell that as well.

Man: SELL THE ALFA ROMEO?

Woman: What difference does any of this make to me?

Man: Oh, fantastic! We're virtually ruined and ...

Woman: You've got loads of money and you're the only one who spends it in any case... I've never even BEEN in the Alfa Romeo so I don't see why any of this is a reason for me to shed tears.

Man: I don't believe this. How can you be so calm?

Woman: I've been expecting it for years, knowing the job you're in and the people you work with.

Man: Yes. You're right, I suppose. I should never have trusted any of them, the...

Woman: Now let me tell you about my day, mmm?

Man: Go on.

Woman: I had a phone call this morning from NLC, you know, the National Lottery?

Man: And?

Woman: I won forty million pounds.

Man: Oh, amazing! Just at the right time! We're saved!

Woman: Well, hang on. I have an appointment this evening to test drive my own Alfa Romeo. And should I decide to buy it, which is more than likely, I shall be straight off down to London with Jane and Christine for a night or two on the town, after which I shall think hard about whether I will be coming back or not. I left some shepherd's pie in the oven. Maybe you'd better not eat it all at once, eh?

Part 1

Question 1

Well, to tell you the truth I was more impressed by the building than the actual event... well, for starters, it wasn't easy to look around. The place was so full of flowers and plants it looked like a jungle. You could easily get lost in there... a machete would have come in handy. It might be a nice set up for the car and boat show... yeah there's one next month. And the humidity! I'm sure they'll have to throw most of the exhibits away when it's finished... humidity destroys electronic equipment, you know.

Question 2

Yes, can you hear me ... I was wondering if you have any ingredients in stock for making Thai curries? Curries, like they do in Thailand... the people in the Thai restaurant said you might have what I need .... ermm coconut milk and lemon grass and... oh, you have that, do you? Oh, good, you were my last hope... the supermarket's got ready-made sauces only... is it fresh or dried? Oh dear, I was hoping for some fresh, I don't suppose you can get it in this country, can you? Never mind, I'll be round soon. OK, thank you.

Question 3

Sorry, Peter, I'm really not clear about that last point. You say that Sally really hates him but she doesn't realise it herself until act three? My feeling is that she's quite clear about her feelings for George by the middle of the second act, that's the office scene... at least that's the way I've been trying to uhmm do it... what do the rest of you think?

Question 4

Erm excuse me madam, but there's a queue... no... no that's just where it turns left, I'm afraid, this is where it ends.... yes practically outside the front door... actually I had to spend some time outside myself ... worse than the supermarket ... you're lucky, it seems there's fewer people coming at this time, or they've got more people on the tills... mmm I think between half an hour and three quarters... oh yes, it's definitely a disgrace, I couldn't agree more, three quarters of an hour for a couple of stamps...

Question 5
Assistant:	Erm I'm sorry madam this is for 10 items or less.
Customer:	Yes, I know.
Assistant:	But you've got much more than that.
Customer:	Can't you count? Pasta, cheese, bread, milk, beer, wine, and toilet rolls... that's seven if my arithmetic doesn't fail me.
Assistant:	Oh no madam, you've misunderstood, it's not the types we count, it's the actual erm pieces... three bottles of beer is three items, you see ...
Customer:	Oh I'm so sorry, I thought.... Well, can I pay here anyway, please... I can't stand another half an hour in the queue.
Assistant:	Well, it's against regulations but all right... That's £ 22.85 please.
Customer:	Here you are.
Assistant:	But, madam... I can't accept cards or cheques here, only cash... I'm afraid you'll have to use one of the others, after all ...

Question 6
Woman:	See, I told you we'd be here with at least an hour to spare.
Man:	Well, better safe than sorry.
Woman:	Will you stop quoting things at me and help me with the luggage?
Man:	Oh, sorry... I could do with a pint or two...
Woman:	Oh great, and then I'll have to spend five hours watching the sheep go by, listening to the soundtrack of your snoring.
Man:	It's not the beer, it's the rocking and the rhythmic sound that does the trick. Anyway, why don't you have a pint yourself?
Woman:	I don't know, I'll get peckish and I can't bear those horrible sandwiches from the buffet car. I told you we should've got the plane:..
Man:	You know we can't afford it... now which platform...

Question 7

Oh he's adorable, a real gentleman ... my grandson has one that looks exactly the same... but not as sweet... whenever we meet it's like he's greeting me the old-fashioned way, you know by tipping his hat and saying 'how do you do'... of course he does it by means of soft barks and wagging his tail gently, none of the jumping around you'd expect... he's a thoroughbred you see, of noble blood... very unlike his master... he can hardly bring himself to say 'hallo'... and we've been neighbours for ages...

Question 8

A: ... I don't like tests, they're boring!

B: Come on, it's not as if it's a maths test or anything, this is fun.

A: But, it's two pages long.

B: Go on, it's a piece of cake, I did it myself yesterday... you just choose one of the options...

A: I told you it's silly, I mean, are these my only options?

B: Now look here, there's psychologists and sociologists behind this test, who're you to criticise it? **A:**

Me   ... and I know myself ... I don't need a silly magazine to tell   **me** *who* I am!

B: Do it anyway, don't you want us to compare?

A: No, not really... this is worse than maths.

Part 2

C: What sort of problems do students have with listening, in your experience, then, Margaret?

M: Well I think the main problem is **PANIC**!

C: Panic?

M: Their teacher switches on a cassette and they expect to understand   every word, and of course that isn't usually possible, so they panic and then they lose the whole message, when they could have understood quite enough to answer the question.

C: Don't they NEED to understand every word?

M: No. We don't listen to *everything* everyone says even in our own language. We usually decide how to listen depending on what we want to know. Do you remember any of the conversations you had yesterday?

C: Yeah, sure.

M: OK, but I bet you remember the subjects and not the exact words, right?

C: Hmmm, yeah...

M: So students need to be aware of *how* to listen... whether they should listen for the overall meaning or for particular details... and you know, in neither case do you need to understand a hundred percent of what you hear.

C: They were all complaining to me about background noise on the cassette the other day...

M: Yes, but again they are not being asked to understand everything, Chris - they can pick out the important information even if the background noise is blocking some other information.

C: So how do you teach them how to listen, then?

M: Well, you need to get them to look at the questions before they listen...

C: Before?

M: Yes, and to decide from the questions if they think they're being asked to listen for overall meaning, such as how the speakers are feeling as they talk, or to understand just the topic of the conversation, or for...

C: Particular information, specific...

M: Yes, specific information such as dates, times, names, places, stuff like that. If they decide beforehand what kind of information they need to listen for, that makes the task a lot easier for them.

C: So, if we do a practice test?

M: Go through the questions with them first, before they hear the cassette, and ask them to guess what kind of information they think they have to listen for. They'll learn to do this for themselves eventually.

C: OK, thanks a lot ... is that cassette recorder working? I had a bit of trouble with it the other day...

Part 3

Speaker 1

Two whole bags of sugar and I don't know how many pounds of blackberries, and it all went up in smoke. I was terrified. I smelled something burning and came rushing downstairs thinking the house was on fire... and there she is in the kitchen saying 'It's all right, mummy, I'm just making some jam, only it isn't ready yet.' I dived past her and switched off the gas. I just managed to stop a disaster.

Speaker 2

You remember the other day, all that rain we had? Well, living in a basement, you get pretty paranoid about rain. I don't know why, but that morning I didn't give it too much thought. I got up and had breakfast and I was just about to leave the house when I noticed the water was coming under the window - the bed was up against the window and all the sheets and the duvet were sodden around the bottom - I managed to unblock the drain and the water went away but imagine if I hadn't noticed it, got back home in the evening and found the place under two feet of water... doesn't bear thinking about.

Speaker 3

I was on a plane from London to Rome, and we were about half an hour out of London when the captain comes on over the speaker, 'Ladies and gentlemen,' he says, all serious, 'We have some bad news for you, I'm afraid.' Can you think about how THAT felt? For a split second you imagine crash landings or bombs or ... anyway they said it was a light on the wings or something that wasn't working and we'd have to turn back to London. That was the 'bad news.' Why he couldn't have said that straight off instead of scaring everybody half to death I don't know.

Speaker 4

I was looking after my niece when she was about two and the phone rang. It was my sister calling from work to say she'd be a bit later than planned picking up my niece. So we were chatting a bit and suddenly there was this enormous crash from behind me. I knew right away what it was... It was the cupboard in the dining room full of plates and glasses and it had fallen over. I shrieked, dropped the phone and found my niece standing in the kitchen looking wide eyed at all the broken plates... but completely safe. My sister was on the other end of the phone in a panic for two whole minutes... I couldn't stop shaking for an hour.

Speaker 5

We heard the fire engines but of course you don't usually take much notice, do you? It was my son's school that was on fire - it's one of those big glass and concrete places and you wouldn't think there would be anything much to burn in one of those, so I didn't think it would have been too traumatic, you know... but he said the windows were exploding and they had to walk down the corridors with their backs pressed to the walls to avoid the smoke and flames... no, absolutely nobody was hurt, but they all got out in just the clothes they stood in... all the kids' books and coats and whatnot got burned.

Part 4

Interviewer:	Please have a seat.
Applicant:	Thank you.
Interviewer:	Now Mr Jones, let me first check that I've got your personal details right. You're Peter M. Jones?
Applicant:	That's right.
Interviewer:	Erm... what does the M stand for?
Applicant:	Mortimer.
Interviewer:	And you're 31?
Applicant:	Erm... 30 actually.
Interviewer:	Now Mr Jones... you were educated at St. Matthew's School and then Midlands University.
Applicant:	Yes I did both my BA and Master's degrees there.
Interviewer:	Mmm, yes, a BA in Economics and an MA in Banking.
Applicant:	Banking & Management actually, my thesis was on management of high-risk loans.
Interviewer:	Mmm yes, very interesting area ... erm... according to my information you didn't do your Master's straight away.
Applicant:	Erm... no I worked for five years for Central Commercial Bank, Manchester office, where I received my initial training.
Interviewer:	I see... can you be more specific about your duties and training at Central Commercial?
Applicant:	Yes of course, well I started at the imports & exports department... my duties were mainly administrative...
Interviewer:	I see, how long did you stay in that position?
Applicant:	For about a year, then I was transferred to the Loans Department where I stayed until my Master's.
Interviewer:	What were your duties there?
Applicant:	After a year's training, I worked at the personal loans and mortgage divisions for two and one year respectively ...
Interviewer:	And after your Master's?
Applicant:	I went to the German Commerce Bank, the London office, where I worked in the high risk loans division.
Interviewer:	You seem to have substantial relevant experience, Mr Jones. Now, can you briefly tell me about your reasons for applying for this position?
Applicant:	I want something more challenging and rewarding, both financially and personally... Sloane's Bank is one of the largest in the world...

Part 1

Question 1

Oh, it really is a ridiculous film, I can't imagine what all the fuss was about when it first came out. This girl is supposed to be possessed by the Devil, or something, and anyway, for most of the film not very much happens and it's all very boring ... mind you I couldn't help laughing at times ... then you get the last thirty minutes of really very unpleasant supernatural sort of stuff, and before you know it, it's all over and nobody has a clue what's supposed to have happened. My boyfriend fainted in front of the telly, but it left me cold.

Question 2

Ooh she makes me crazy.... you know that way she's got of talking to you as if you were a naughty child? As I was leaving, she says to me, "Janet, is that your computer?" meaning - well, of course it's the computer I use, we both know that, "Is that your computer?" meaning, of course, "could you switch your computer off before you go?" So why can't she just SAY that, instead of being so patronizing?

Question 3

Yeah, it was a really friendly place when they first opened a few years ago, but it has really gone downhill nowadays. They were always very welcoming, and they were always giving you free beers, then for some reason people didn't go any more, it got a bit expensive after that, and now you go in and it's really quiet, just the two of them sitting there looking miserable, no wonder nobody wants to drink there any more.

Question 4

Well, there's nothing obviously wrong, Mr. Porter. I think the problem is, you've been overdoing it. I suggest you try to cut out the cigarettes and the whisky and try to get some rest. Can you take a holiday? Or at least take a little time off work to come round a bit? I can give you a note, that's not a problem. A rest will be a lot better for you than tablets, I'm sure.

Question 5

M: Does anyone want anything from the kiosk?
W: Twenty Marlboro and a bar of chocolate, I don't care what sort. Do you want the money now?
M: No, give it to me when I get back. Do I owe you anything from the other day?
W: What for?
M: That's what I'm asking.
W: What did you have the other day?
M: I can't remember.
W: In that case, yes, you owe me three pounds fifty.

Question 6

He's a vegetarian, this friend of our Diane's.... no, no meat or fish... so what do they eat, then? She's bringing him for lunch this Sunday... Well, George won't like that, not a bit, I can tell you... yogurt and nuts for Sunday lunch when he's used to roast beef. What do they eat apart from yogurt and nuts then, or is that just for pudding?... Mushroom omelettes sounds nice but Claire won't eat mushrooms and Diane's allergic to eggs... tofu?... never heard of it, where do you get tofu from? Hmmm. Might be a problem.......

Question 7

Can somebody answer the phone..... I'm in the bath! Why is it this house falls apart if I'm not there to supervise absolutely everything?... Who keeps turning the kitchen taps on all the time, there won't be any hot water to rinse my hair... and will you please put on a different CD because we've heard that one three times in a row already .... or NO CD AT ALL, that'd suit me fine... ohh and why can't you all just go out for the evening and leave me in peace for a change?

Question 8

This morning I would like to go over one or two points that I think need clearing up. Let's begin with using the photocopier..... If you want photocopies, please remember to ask the secretary as far in advance as you can, and please, not do them yourself? We can't have everybody using the copier, it's far too fragile these days and we can't afford a new one yet. .. Sorry? ... No, I'm afraid you can't ask your teacher, either...... They've got enough copying to do for themselves. ... Secondly, can you please, please, call if you're going to be absent...

Part 2

Good afternoon and welcome to another edition of 'You and your body'. The topic of today's programme is vitamins, one of the basic components of the human body, and one that still mystifies many people ... at least that's what the letters from listeners show. Today we will try to answer as many of your questions as possible.

So... what are vitamins? Well, vitamins are one of the five elements essential for a healthy body ... the others are proteins - which we get from meat, carbohydrates - which we get from pasta and bread, fats, and minerals. Actually the name vitamin comes from Latin vita which means 'life'.

Now, before we go on, let me clarify something. Some people may believe that vitamins and minerals are similar because they're combined in the various food supplements on the market... but they're not. Vitamins are organic compounds, whereas minerals are inorganic substances. For example calcium is a mineral not a vitamin.

Actually, even vitamins differ from one another in their chemical composition and the way they act. Nevertheless, we can see two main vitamin groups: fat-soluble and water-soluble... that is vitamins that can dissolve either into fat or into water. Let's have a closer look at those two groups.

Fat soluble are vitamins A, D, E, and K. Their common characteristic is that the body can store them in fat, in the liver and in the kidneys. So we don't need to take them on a daily basis.

Water-soluble are vitamin C and the vitamin B complex. The body cannot store them, so we must make sure that they are contained in our daily diet.

Why are vitamins so important? The main reason is that vitamins help the metabolism of three of the important elements we mentioned before: proteins, carbohydrates, and fats. In other words, without vitamins the body cannot process these essential substances. Vitamins also help the body create blood cells, hormones, chemicals in the nervous system and genetic material. Unfortunately, we still don't know much about the complex ways in which vitamins operate in the body. Actually, we are not even sure about the precise effect of certain vitamins, for example vitamin E.

You may be asking 'How do we get these vital elements?' Well, the main sources of vitamins are just around the corner at your local supermarket. We can see two categories: plant products such as fresh fruit & vegetables; vegetable oil and margarine; bread, pasta & cereals; and animal products: meat, poultry & fish; liver, heart & kidneys; and dairy products, that is fresh milk, butter and cheese. Now, there is one vitamin which you get for free, so to speak. Most of vitamin D is produced in the body when the skin is exposed to sunlight. And here is an important piece of information for vegetarians who don't eat any animal products. Because vitamin B12 is found only in animal products vegans should take vitamin B12 supplements. Vitamin supplements may also be needed by pregnant women and people on special diets.

I would like to end this programme with a word of caution. Vitamins are essential for our health and we do need to ensure that we take the necessary amounts, but we can have too much of a good thing. Yes, it may sound strange to some of you, but taking more than the amount we need will result in a number of health problems. This happens particularly with fat-soluble vitamins. For example, large amounts of vitamin A can cause anything from headaches and skin rashes to growth problems in children. Even large doses of vitamin C, which is not stored in the body, can destroy vitamin B12 and reduce calcium in bones. So be careful when taking food supplements. Good day and Good health....

Part 3

Speaker 1
Hi, it's me ...look, I know it's going to sound like the most ridiculous excuse but it's the truth ...I was on time, really I was, only – and I know this is going to be difficult to believe, ermm... it seems I forgot to jot down the name. I thought you said the Plaza... so there I am thinking I was early when I realise that the film was just about to start ...so I thought 'oh no I'm late' and rushed into the cinema thinking I was going to find you inside – at least at the intermission ... I realised just now and I'm calling to explain...

Speaker 2
Hi Bill, it's me ...I'm calling to say I'm sorry about this evening ...it's been one of those days ...panic in the office ...I managed to escape just in time ...almost missed the bus and just as I thought it was safe to relax and was looking forward to the evening, the traffic virtually comes to a standstill ...there was an accident and the junction was clogged ...after doing 100 metres in 10 minutes I decided to get off and get a taxi ...but you know how things are... when you really need one... sorry again... please call me.

Speaker 3
Ermm... hi it's Celia... I'm calling to explain about yesterday... I'm sure you'll understand – I had a little accident on my way to the cinema – I'm perfectly OK, which is something I can't say about the car... My watch was slow you see and when I realised what time it was, I was rather late... I was driving a bit too fast and wasn't really concentrating, as you can imagine and... well... I didn't see the bus... Fortunately the driver saw me, but still the damage... anyway I shouldn't bother you with that... let's arrange something for this evening

Speaker 4

Hi James it's me ..I know, I know ...where was I... well let me tell you, and then we can think about selling the rights to Hollywood... now my watch was fast – only I hadn't noticed... so I thought I had left home rather late... I drove like mad... I nearly bumped into a bus... I was very lucky... but finally I managed to be there on time – or so I thought... so I waited for almost an hour wondering what had happened to you... I must have left minutes before you arrived... am I forgiven?

Speaker 5
Hi Jenny, I tried to call you earlier but you weren't in and there seemed to be something funny with the answering machine so I couldn't leave a message... I'm terribly sorry, but I couldn't help it... there was a power cut last night and my alarm clock is electric, so it didn't go off... ermm that's when I tried to call you but... anyway it was impossible to find a taxi... so I took the bus, but with the traffic being the usual mess I couldn't make it on time... I'll make it up to you I promise... I'll call you again later, bye...

Part 4

Interviewer:	Hallo, today we are going to hear about a new chain of stores that aims to revolutionise video rental. In the studio we have with us Mike Mulligan, the man behind Computer Video Rental or CVR. Now Mike, what is unique about this new type of store?
Mulligan:	Erm, quite a lot I would say. But let me start with what our customers will find familiar. Now, at first glance a CVR store looks like any conventional store of its kind. It has got video tapes and laser discs displayed by topic, plus special categories for famous actors & directors and award-winning films. So customers can come and browse the 'traditional way', too.
Interviewer:	I see, so where does the 'computer' element come in?
Mulligan:	Well, to start with, all film titles are stored in a computer, which is connected to a number of terminals. Customers can ask the computer to display film titles that match a number of characteristics.
Interviewer:	What are these characteristics?
Mulligan:	For each film the computer has information about the type of film - comedy, thriller, etc - the story, the names of the main characters, the date it was released, the leading actors, the director, the scriptwriter, any awards it has won, and of course the title.
Interviewer:	How is this helpful? Can you give us an example?
Mulligan:	Well, let's say that you have heard of a good film, but can't remember the title; you only remember that it's a thriller and the story. You type thriller and some key words from the story, and the computer finds the film for you.
Interviewer:	Impressive, but isn't it rather complicated?
Mulligan:	Well, customers can always ask our well-trained staff for help or they can find the video the traditional way.
Interviewer:	But people still have to come to the store.
Mulligan:	Oh no, members can order video tapes or laser discs by phone, fax or even electronic mail, and we will deliver them within 30 minutes... for a fee of course.
Interviewer:	Well, it seems that after pizza delivery we'll have to get used to video delivery now. I understand that Computer Video Rental stores are open 24 hours a day, 7 days a week., don't you **ever** close?
Mulligan:	Only from 8 pm on New Year's Eve to 8 am, January 2nd.
Interviewer:	Well, video renting will never be the same again.
Mulligan:	That's the idea. Actually we have plans to introduce a CD section in our stores.
Interviewer:	Well, music stores beware... I'd like to thank Mike Mulligan of CVR stores...

Part 1

Question 1
It'd make life a lot easier if I didn't have the cat. Well... in some ways. I mean, she's adorable and I couldn't bear not to have her around, but it's difficult if you have to go away for any length of time, finding someone to come and feed her or having to fork out a fortune for the cattery fees. And it can really restrict you looking for a new place to live... like I am now. There has to be a balcony or a yard outside so she can get out and run around - she'd go mad if she had nowhere to play - and she'd probably wreck the furniture into the bargain.

Question 2
It started as a functional but expensive tool for professionals and people in high positions. Because of this, it became a status symbol, and as its price started decreasing due to cheaper technology, more and more people started carrying one, not because they really needed to be reached at any time, but because of the status it was supposed to afford them. In other words, it became more like a piece of jewellery. Unlike jewels though, as more and more people are able to afford one, it will no longer symbolise wealth and power but it will become a tool again. Its evolution resembles other technological advancements of the past like the radio and the conventional cable phone, of which we can say it is a combination.

Question 3
"...very nice little kitchen here, just been painted. We'll get the fridge fixed, no problem... Yes, the bathroom's next door... oh, that's from the hot tap, it does leak a bit, but we'll soon have that sorted out, though. No, there's no garden out in the back, basement flats tend not to have one, but it's nice and cool in summer and nice and warm in winter... It is a pleasant sitting room, isn't it?... Just been painted and decorated... beg your pardon? Well, yes, you can if you don't like them, but they *are* brand new, I've just had them put in, just put them away in a cupboard or something... so? What do you think? Can we come to some arrangement...?"

Question 4
A: The thing's stuck again. And look how they're coming out... all black.
B: Turn that knob round, the one with the thing that looks like a sun on it.
A: Oh, that's better, but they still look a bit dark ...
B: That's because the cover's not completely down.
A: The book's too thick, you can't close it properly.
B: Put a jacket over the whole thing.
A: Oh, what a mess!... can't we just take them down to the shop and get them done there?

Question 5
It isn't anything like I expected. I thought it would be really boring and dry, you know, like being back at school and having loads of reading and writing to do and these really sarcastic teachers. What's more I'd heard some quite off-putting comments from a couple of colleagues who'd done the course and I was very sceptical... but I thought I'd give it a go. I'm glad I did.

Question 6
Good morning, Mrs Greenaway? It's Julie here, from Stafford and Cripps, how are you? Yes, fine, thank you... I had a message from Mrs Boyle, I believe you had an appointment this coming Wednesday... Wednesday, that's... you did? Yes, well she was wondering if you wouldn't mind some time later, if that's ok with you... What with you coming from so far away, the other end of the city and all... perhaps you would like to make it later in the day or even on another day... Yes... ok, lovely, just a couple of hours later then, and you're both happier. Yes, well... bye for now then, yes okay... Bye.

Question 7
... in front of five thousand very amused spectators. It appears the referee's foot was caught in a rope on the side of the pool while he was running .... he executed some delicate ballerina-like movements trying to regain his balance before he fell over into the pool, waving hands and feet wildly in the air, just like a cartoon character. But what caused most of the audience to practically fall off their seats with laughter was that throughout this whole choreography he had his whistle in his mouth ...

Question 8
Are you coming by bus or by taxi? By bus you have to take the 54, get off at the big supermarket at the corner of Ramsden Street and walk the rest of the way - a total of about twenty minutes - if you get a taxi tell them to let you out at the bottom of Castle Hill and walk the rest of the way - quarter of an hour or so, I'd say - but because traffic will be busy at that time of day and it'll take you ages, and cost you an arm and a leg... cost me about twelve quid

last time... it might be easier and faster if you walked, so... it's up to you... take your pick.

Part 2

Good evening and welcome to another lecture in our 'Science in Simple Terms' series. This evening Dr. Edward Pickering will talk about a very popular topic, Dinosaurs.

Ermm... thank you. Let me start by saying that there is still a lot to discover about dinosaurs. Everything we know is based on the fossils ... ermm... let's say the skeletons we have found. So, as new evidence is discovered our view of dinosaurs changes. We palaeontologists don't even agree amongst ourselves... So, I will try to present what we generally agree on, without using complicated scientific terms.

First of all, we need to understand that not all animals which lived millions of years ago, were dinosaurs. Dinosaurs were only one of many species, ermm... types of animals. For example the pterodactyls and woolly mammoths were not dinosaurs. ... So what were dinosaurs? Dinosaurs were reptiles... ermm... examples of modern-day reptiles are snakes and lizards. Actually their name comes from Greek and means 'terrible lizard'.

It is also important to understand that dinosaurs were not a single type of animal, but a whole family, which included hundreds of types of quite different sizes, shapes, colours and behaviours... ermm... in the same way as the family of Mammals includes humans, dogs, whales and bats.

Dinosaurs are divided into two large groups: 'bird-hipped' and 'lizard-hipped' according to the way the bones were connected to their hips, **not** because they looked like birds or lizards themselves.

Their sizes ranged quite a lot. The smallest was the size of a pigeon and weighed only a few grams. The biggest was about 26m long, twice as tall as an elephant and weighed about 20 times as much.

Let's have a look now at their habits and behaviour. Well, despite a popular myth, dinosaurs were not all meat-eaters. Bird-hipped dinosaurs were herbivores, that is they ate only plants, and lizard-hipped dinosaurs were either meat or plant eaters. Plant eating dinosaurs were larger than meat-eaters. Some of the smaller meat-eaters probably hunted in groups.

Dinosaurs only lived on land, or in some cases in areas with shallow water. They laid eggs, and probably built nests at the same place every year.

Regarding their intelligence... overall dinosaurs are thought to have been as intelligent as modern-day reptiles for example, crocodiles. In the beginning it was believed that they weren't intelligent creatures because their brains were rather small - but this was not a good indicator. What is important is not the actual size, but the relation of the size of the brain to the size of the animal. Their brain size varied according to types and seems to have been larger in small meat-eating types.

Dinosaurs appeared about 200 million years ago and became extinct .. ermm... disappeared 65 million years ago. That is, they ruled the earth for almost 140 million years. To help you understand how long that is let me tell you that humans have only existed for about 2 million years.

Why did they disappear? No-one knows for certain. There are many theories about the cause, but most of them have to do more with fantasy than reality. The theory that a meteor which supposedly hit the earth 65 million years ago caused dramatic changes in the climate is not impossible, but has two drawbacks. First, it is rather odd that only dinosaurs were affected, as we have evidence that other animals (e.g. crocodiles, fishes and birds) were affected very little. Second, most types of dinosaurs had already died out by that time. The most plausible theory is that they disappeared gradually over the course of millions of years because the climate changed. An almost stable climate all year round was gradually replaced by seasons with bigger and bigger variations in temperature and rainfall. Not being able to adapt, dinosaurs (among other types of animals) died out gradually.

But are dinosaurs completely extinct? Well, surprisingly enough, no. Their descendants, birds, are still around. It may be hard to believe, but it's true; birds evolved from a specific type of dinosaur ... funnily enough from a meat-eating 'lizard-hipped' type.

Part 3

Speaker 1
I'm only telling you what I saw, that's all, and you can make of it what you want. The statue moved - she raised her hands and moved her head... only slightly, but it was obvious to anybody watching that the statue really did move... like a real person. I said, I haven't a clue how it happened. I didn't say it was possible - I just say it happened.

Speaker 2
I saw it move, but I'm not convinced it really did. You know, they had the statue in the church and there must have been hundreds of candles around it. The light from the candles and the heat coming from them, makes things sort of shimmer and you can think they're moving but it... I don't know, I think it's possibly the effect of the heat and the light.

Speaker 3
I saw nothing myself but lots of people say they saw the statue move more than once. Maybe they did. You have a big crowd of people in a church and they're all waiting for a miracle to happen. There's this tremendous

atmosphere of expectation. I don't think it's surprising that people start to see things - after all, they desperately want to in most cases.

Speaker 4
I've been all over the world looking for this type of phenomenon - there's always a statue somewhere that's supposed to cry, or sing, or move and you get people flocking to see a miracle - like I say I've been all over the place hoping to see this sort of thing. And I've never once seen a statue so much as wobble. Maybe I'm just unlucky, or more likely, we're all being fooled.

Speaker 5
Why do they want miracles? They flock in here night after night waiting for the statue to move, as though a moving statue had any meaning at all... I mean, is there nothing they could be doing? Sick people to help? Homeless children to take care of? There's a whole world of suffering out there and they're all stuck in that nice warm church...

Part 4

Int:	Welcome to Vocational Orientation. Every week three members of a specific profession present its positive and negative aspects. Today we're going to examine nursing, and as we do every week we're going to try and answer your questions. So, let's start with qualifications. Nick?
Nick:	I think Jane is better qualified to answer this, as she's also involved in training nurses.
Jane:	Ermm, ok.. To become a nurse now you need to attend college for 3 years, but you also need to gain practical experience working in hospitals... under supervision of course.
Int:	Was it different when you started?
Jane:	Yes, it was mainly practical training then, ermm... 25 years ago.
Int:	How do you feel about this Peggy?
Peggy:	I wish it had stayed the same... I could have done without some of the lessons at college... I learned so much more at the hospital.
Nick:	I don't agree, I think the lessons at college helped me make the most of my practical training.
Peggy:	I don't know... maybe it's just me... I don't really care much for studying ... tell you what though, having to go to college has helped the status of nursing - somehow...
Jane:	Hasn't done my paycheque much good though. (laughs)
Int:	What about duties?
Jane:	Ermm... this depends on experience and special training. In the beginning duties involve bathing patients, administering medicine, taking blood pressure and so on...
Nick:	Which came as an anticlimax for me... I don't know, possibly I expected too much too soon. What about you Peggy?
Peggy:	I wasn't thrilled either, but it didn't bother me, I was expecting it actually.
Jane:	Later on nurses take on more responsibilities ... and they can also specialise... actually in the last few years nurses have been allowed to perform duties which were formerly reserved only for doctors.
Peggy:	I'm not too keen on that actually, Jane. I'd rather follow doctors' directions... I feel safer.
Nick:	But that's exactly why a college education is so important now... it gives us new career prospects...
Int:	What about the hours?
Jane:	Well, it's not a nine to five job that's for sure. It's a job that requires a lot of stamina...
Peggy:	... and nerves of steel
Jane:	... but it's fulfilling... it's nice to know that you can help.
Nick:	Not that everybody values what we do... Ok it's our job, but a simple thank you can go a long way.
Peggy:	I think people do show their appreciation - possibly you expect too much.
Nick:	... and I hate it when some people look disappointed when they see me - I mean is caring exclusively a female quality?
Peggy:	You shouldn't take it personally... I think it's expected... traditionally nurses have been women, I mean think of Florence Nightingale... it's possibly a stereotype you should learn to live with... women have to cope with much worse.
Jane:	That's a rather far fetched approach... I do think Nick is overreacting, but he's got a point ...